This book belong to:

Bob Hedges

DECEMBER 25 2005 (FROM MUM)

THE SOUTH WALES MAIN LINE

PART FOUR
BRIDGEND (WEST) TO SWANSEA

BY
JOHN HODGE

Canton 'Britannia' No. 70015 *Apollo* bringing the 1.55 p.m. Paddington to Swansea into Swansea High Street station on 20th May 1958. Portions for Pembroke Dock, Fishguard and Neyland were at the head of the train, with the Swansea section, including a dining pair, at the rear; the latter would be removed first, and taken to the coach sidings for use the following morning on the 8.0 a.m. Neyland (10.30 a.m. Swansea).
NORMAN SIMMONDS/HUGH DAVIES

WILD SWAN PUBLICATIONS

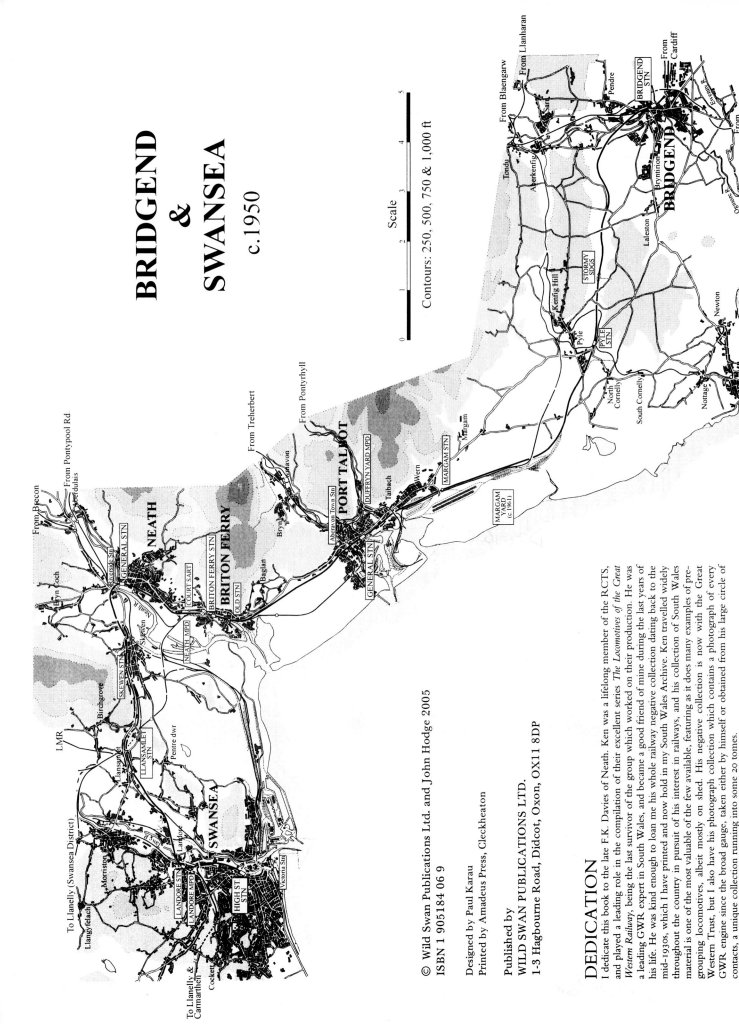

BRIDGEND & SWANSEA c.1950

Scale

Contours: 250, 500, 750 & 1,000 ft

0 1 2 3 4 5

© Wild Swan Publications Ltd. and John Hodge 2005
ISBN 1 905184 06 9

Designed by Paul Karau
Printed by Amadeus Press, Cleckheaton

Published by
WILD SWAN PUBLICATIONS LTD.
1-3 Hagbourne Road, Didcot, Oxon, OX11 8DP

DEDICATION

I dedicate this book to the late F.K. Davies of Neath. Ken was a lifelong member of the RCTS, and played a leading role in the compilation of their excellent series *The Locomotives of the Great Western Railway*, being the last survivor of the group which worked on their production. He was a leading GWR expert in South Wales, and became a good friend of mine during the last years of his life. He was kind enough to loan me his whole railway negative collection dating back to the mid-1930s, which I have printed and now hold in my South Wales Archive. Ken travelled widely throughout the country in pursuit of his interest in railways, and his collection of South Wales material is one of the most valuable of the few available, featuring as it does many examples of pre-grouping locomotives, albeit mostly on shed. His negative collection is now with the Great Western Trust, but I also have his photograph collection which contains a photograph of every GWR engine since the broad gauge, taken either by himself or obtained from his large circle of contacts, a unique collection running into some 20 tomes.

Map labels

NEATH

BRITON FERRY

PORT TALBOT

SWANSEA

BRIDGEND

GENERAL STN

RIVERSIDE STN

COURT SART

BRITON FERRY STN

OLD STN

NEATH MPD

SKEWEN STN

LLANSAMLET STN

LANDORE STN

LANDORE MPD

HIGH ST STN

VICTORIA STN

DUFFRYN YARD MPD

GENERAL STN

ABERAVON TOWN STN

MARGAM STN

MARGAM YARD (c.1961)

STORMY SDGS

PYLE STN

BRIDGEND STN

From Brecon
From Pontypool Rd.
From Treherbert
From Pontyrhyll
From Blaengarw
From Llanharan
From Cardiff
From Barry

To Llanelly (Swansea District)
To Llanelly & Carmarthen

Llangyfelach
Morriston
Birchgrove
Bryn Coch
Cwmdulais
Cockett
Bryn
Baglan
Wern
Taibach
Margam
Pyle
North Cornelly
South Cornelly
Nottage
Newton
Porthcawl
Laleston
Kenfig Hill
Pendre
Sant
Tondu
Aberkenfig
Bryntirion
Pentre dwr
Skewen
Tirisaf
Llandore
Llansamlet
Cwmavon
Aberavon

LMR
Ogmore R.
Ewenny R.

PREFACE

With hindsight, I always wish I had done more to record the railway scene at places of interest in South Wales, but, for once, I am fairly happy with my coverage of the main locations featured in this volume. I visited Port Talbot during the rebuilding of the station, which I recorded on film one sunny weekday afternoon when traffic was brisk; Briton Ferry on a couple of occasions, where I walked to a few very good vantage points for photography; Neath on a dull day, when photographic success is in the lap of the gods; and spent several afternoons at Swansea (High Street), where I recorded the limited number of views from the east end of the platforms. I hope the end product produces a comprehensive and balanced view of the Bridgend to Swansea section of the South Wales Main Line to complement the other three volumes so far produced.

A stopping passenger train waiting at the Down Main platform, Port Talbot, behind Ebbw Jct. 'Grange' No. 6868 *Penrhos Grange* on 27th March 1948. This engine was transferred to Taunton three months later. The station then had separate up and down platforms, with bays at the 'west' end of each, although there were no independent freight lines running through the station at this time.

F. K. DAVIES, CTY GW TRUST

Canton's curved-frame 'Bulldog' No. 3303 *St. Anthony* heading an up 8-coach stopping train through Skewen in 1929. This service may have been the 11.20 a.m. Carmarthen (12.30 p.m. Swansea) to Bristol, which was due to pass the 8.55 a.m. Paddington around Skewen.

F. R. HEBRON – RAIL ARCHIVE STEPHENSON

INTRODUCTION

The South Wales Railway opened their line from Chepstow to Swansea in 1850, continuing from Landore to New Milford in 1852. With Brunel as engineer, the line fulfilled the Great Western's overall plan to create a railway to connect London with Southern Ireland via a West Wales port, and onward steamer transport across the Irish Sea.

Between Chepstow and Swansea, the line ran through reasonably easily-worked terrain, except for the Newport, Neath and Landore areas. It was punctuated on its seaward side by a series of modest, but developing, docks, the first at Newport, and another at Cardiff both set to become major installations in their own right. Beyond Cardiff, the line ran through a more rural environment, but after Margam, it once again met up with docklands, though on a smaller scale, as it passed near Aberavon, Briton Ferry and Neath. The line finally reached the town of Swansea, which was on a par with Newport and Cardiff in terms of dock development and included a sizeable viaduct over the Tawe at Landore.

When the prospectus for the SWR was issued in 1844, it contained a proposal for the section of the route from Bridgend to run initially south-westwards along the coastal plain, which it was to follow around to Aberavon, but this was rejected as being too close to the shifting sands near Newton Nottage (later Newton, to the east of Porthcawl). The line of route was thus changed to run further inland, north-westwards via Pyle and Margam, and although this was three miles shorter than the original proposal, it did involve significant gradients in the climb to Stormy Down, particularly in the eastwards direction. This legacy was carried forward, and became the main operating restriction between Swansea and Cardiff right through the age of steam traction in South Wales that lasted until 1965.

Having passed through the rural landscape between Bridgend and Pyle, the new railway reached an area that would, in the course of time, develop into one of the main areas of heavy industry in South Wales, principally around the town of Port Talbot. Even at its opening, the railway regularly encountered iron, copper and tin works, and collieries alongside this part of its route.

In addition to the problems which led to the revised route between Bridgend and Margam, there were further significant engineering aspects to be overcome. The first was the crossing of the River Neath. Brunel's original plans for the South Wales Railway had envisaged a line following the coast around from Briton Ferry towards Swansea, crossing the River Neath by means of a substantial bridge. However, the inhabitants of Neath objected on the grounds that a bridge across the mouth of the river would considerably damage their shipping trade, whilst the town would not be directly served by the proposed main line. The existing route via Neath, Skewen and Landore was taken instead, with a rather more modest crossing of the river to the north-west of the town.

Further west, the crossing of the River Tawe, the Swansea Canal and the surrounding marshland was probably the greatest single impediment on the whole project, and produced a timber viaduct 599 yards long. This structure was rebuilt in the late 1880s, and again in the 1970s.

Landore viaduct, pictured c.1887 looking towards Swansea, and seen largely in its original 1850s form. At around its mid-point can be seen the raised bridgework portion, where the River Tawe was crossed. This viaduct was in the process of being replaced, and signs of work are already evident around the base. In this, the eastern part of the structure leading up to the river was removed and replaced by an embankment, whilst a new viaduct was constructed for the river crossing and the portion into Landore station, located in the far distance. The first of the masonry piers can be seen under construction for the river crossing, and probably indicates the starting point of the new viaduct.   NATIONAL RAILWAY MUSEUM

A view of the Skewen Arches showing Old Oak Common 'Castle' No. 4076 *Carmarthen Castle*, already equipped with a Collett 4,000-gallon tender, at the head of the 12.45 p.m. Neyland (3.55 p.m. Swansea) to Paddington service in 1929. From Swansea, this train carried 'A' headlamps, being a local service up to that point. The leading coach, a clerestory brake third with a large van area, was the first of the three vehicles conveyed from Swansea to Swindon, whilst the Neyland to Paddington portion, fitted with roofboards is seen behind.

F. R. HEBRON – RAIL ARCHIVE STEPHENSON

A Wolverhampton Division '43 XX' 2–6–0 No. 5355 passing under Skewen Arches with the seven-coach 3.50 p.m. Swansea to Cardiff and Hereford service in 1929. During that year, No. 5355 was at Oxley shed, then transferred to Tyseley, whose engines worked a long diagram to Carmarthen; on its return journey, the engine (often a 'Saint') took the 11.10 a.m. Milford to Paddington train from Carmarthen (12.50 p.m.) to Swansea High St, and the 3.50 p.m. to Hereford thence.
F. R. HEBRON – RAIL ARCHIVE STEPHENSON

From Landore, the line turned sharply to the south to follow the River Tawe into Swansea, and terminated at a station near High St. Meanwhile, the through route to Llanelly and Carmarthen, opened onwards from Landore in October 1852, continued on a generally westerly heading. The main line thus avoided the centre of Swansea by around a mile, and it was necessary to provide full facilities at the junction station of Landore, from where branch line operations served the town.

The line throughout was constructed using bridge rails laid on longitudinal timbers, Brunel's usual pattern of construction, and the signalling was of the disc and crossbar type. Engines and rolling stock for the whole of the South Wales Railway were provided by the Great Western and, as the line was initially marooned west of Grange Court, south-west of Gloucester, these had to be shipped across from Bristol. Unfortunately, as often happens in these circumstances, the quality of many of the engines provided was not particularly good, and this was soon to cause problems in working coal traffic between Neath and Swansea, where an incline to Skewen proved prohibitive, and led to the Vale of Neath company working their own traffic, and later building their own line.

In terms of gradient profile, the down line from Bridgend to Swansea was not a difficult stretch. Following a climb at 1 in 132 westwards from Bridgend to Laleston and the 1 in 163 to Stormy Down summit, there was an easy run down the other side of Stormy through Pyle. As the flatlands of Margam Moors were reached, the line entered the acrid and smut-laden air of industrial Port Talbot, and continued on the level through further areas of heavy industry at Briton Ferry and Neath. There was then a climb at 1 in 99 rising to 1 in 88 to Skewen, but then it was downhill again to Swansea Valley Junction with only a small rise on to Landore before turning left downhill again into Swansea High Street.

Train crews faced a stiff climb in the up direction from High Street to Landore, including a short spell at 1 in 37. There was then a further climb at 1 in 106 to Llansamlet, with a short spell of 1 in 91 before levelling out through Skewen and enjoying the first spell of downhill running to Neath. Then it was an easy run along the flat to Margam Moors before the 1 in 139 to Pyle, and the long drag at 1 in 93 to Stormy summit, which required bankers for freight trains. Once over the top at Stormy, it was downhill all the way to Bridgend, and but for the climb to Llanharan, the fireman could have enjoyed the rural scenery all the way to Cardiff!

CONNECTIONS & CROSSINGS

In its development beyond Bridgend, the South Wales Railway made connections with other, local railway companies. However, at the beginning, few connections were made, and only the Vale of Neath provided a significant link outside the Great Western sphere.

In geographical sequence, the first of the connections encountered out of Bridgend was the Llynfi Valley Railway, authorised in 1846, which built a broad gauge railway from Bridgend to Tywith (Nantyffyllon), connecting with the South Wales Railway at Bridgend, and opened for traffic in August 1861 by a junction a short distance to the west of Bridgend station. This line was converted to mixed gauge in 1865.

During 1829, the Duffryn, Llynvi & Porthcawl Railway had opened a horse-drawn tramway between Nantyffyllon and the port of Porthcawl, which crossed the new main line on the level a short distance to the east of Pyle. In 1847, this company was acquired by the Llynfi Valley Railway, which itself was re-incorporated and authorised for working by locomotive power in 1855. Until 1864, a short connecting curve was in operation from the branch to the main line, leaving the branch just to the north of the main line curving around eastwards to Llynvi (later Stormy) Jct. on the main line. This was used to bring coal to a transfer station located near the site of the later Stormy Sidings. The level crossing of the main line was removed in 1876 and the branch taken underneath, with an enlarged-radius curve installed. The branch swung westwards to gently converge with the main line in the vicinity of Pyle, where a connection to the Great Western line was made, also in 1876.

The Llynfi company was amalgamated with the Ogmore Valley Railway to become the Llynfi & Ogmore in 1866, which in turn was amalgamated with the Great Western in 1883.

A couple of miles to the west of Pyle, the Port Talbot Railway & Docks line from Cefn Jct. (where it connected with the Tondu & Porthcawl line) crossed over the main line en route to Margam and Port Talbot. This line also had a connection from Waterhall Jct. to the main line at Pyle, entering that station from the north. This section of the Port Talbot line was a very late addition to the railway scene, being opened in December 1898.

Another line of the Port Talbot company crossed over the main on the southern outskirts of that town before descending to join with the Cefn line as it approached the docks – this was the 'main line' from Pont-y-Rhyll. There was a connection between the South Wales and Port Talbot companies just to the south of Port Talbot station, and another further still to the south, in the vicinity of the original Margam Sidings.

There were also a number of minor mineral lines in the area in the earlier days, one of which – the Oakwood Mineral Railway – crossed the main line on the level immediately to the south of Port Talbot station's platforms on its way into the docks. This crossing was abolished in the years before the Great War.

Another company serving Port Talbot was the Rhondda & Swansea Bay Railway. This opened in November 1885 with a line from nearby Aberavon running north-eastwards to Cymmer, extended on to Treherbert five years later. A direct effect on the South Wales main line was felt in December 1893, when the westwards extension of the line from Aberavon R & SB station crossed over on the level, a short distance to the north of Port Talbot station. The R & SB line then turned north and paralleled the main line, running between it and the coast until the southern approaches to Briton Ferry, when it crossed underneath the main line to its own station alongside the Great Western's. In December 1894, the R & SB line was extended beyond its station at Briton Ferry to run parallel with the GWR line, this time on its inland side, for a mile or so to Court Sart, where the line turned west and once more crossed beneath the main line on its own way into Swansea.

The South Wales Mineral Railway was created in 1853, when four small companies built a broad gauge line to connect with the South Wales Railway, some 12 miles in length between Glyncorrwg Colliery and Briton Ferry, opened in 1861. This line crossed over the main line just to the south of Court Sart, with connections to the R & SB line to Swansea (from its opening in 1894), and to the SWR/GWR goods lines into Briton Ferry docks.

At Neath, the Vale of Neath Railway – opened in 1851, initially to Aberdare – made a connection with the South Wales Railway to the north of the station, using running powers to work its own traffic through to both Swansea and Briton Ferry Docks. This line was extended by the Taff Vale Extension Railway (West Midland Railway, ex-Newport, Abergavenny & Hereford) to Pontypool Road by 1864. The company found their own way into Swansea Harbour from 1863 by the Swansea & Neath Railway, amalgamated with the Vale of Neath company in 1863, although in later years passenger traffic reverted to the GWR line.

Further west, between Llansamlet and Landore, the main line was crossed on the level by the Swansea Vale Railway on its way from the industrial valleys north of Swansea, through Six Pit Junction to Swansea Docks. This dangerous junction produced a collision between trains on the two lines in October 1856, and this speeded up the decision by the SVR to burrow the local line under the main line, a development completed in February 1857. There was no initial connection between the two lines, but in later years

a junction was created (Swansea Valley Junction) just to the west, to enable through running between the two lines.

In June 1852, the Swansea Coal branch was opened from a junction just outside High Street station to serve the North Dock, where basic coal shipment facilities were available.

The South Wales Railway amalgamated with the Great Western Railway in August 1863, and from then on the system began to enjoy the benefits of being part of one of the country's principal transport concerns. The problems created by the need to tranship loads between broad and narrow gauge wagons for onward conveyance to locations served by other than the South Wales and Great Western Railways posed considerable operational and economic problems, and in 1872 the GWR converted the whole of their line from Swindon to New Milford to the narrow gauge. The last broad gauge train ran on Saturday, 11th May, truly a milestone in the development of transport in South Wales. As traffic levels increased, additional sidings were laid in at locations along the main line to hold and marshal both the forwarded and received traffic, especially in those industrial and dock areas which were to become the lifeblood of the industrial scene in that area. New signal boxes were required, both to work the new type of block post and semaphore signalling which soon replaced the original disc and crossbar, and to provide for the many new connections between the main and subsidiary lines. The railway had become the biggest employer in the area, alongside the docks.

PASSENGER TRAFFIC

The original purpose of the South Wales Main Line had been to provide a direct link between London and Southern Ireland via New Milford (Neyland). It was not surprising, therefore, that as time progressed, the GWR afforded huge importance to those services, occasionally at the expense of points en route.

Passenger services over the line in 1856 amounted to five through trains daily, including one express each way that called only at Bridgend, Port Talbot, Neath and Landore (for Swansea). There were three through trains on Sundays in each direction, plus a 'short' service between Swansea and Neath. With the extension of the line to the west of Landore as far as Carmarthen in 1852, Haverfordwest in 1854 and New Milford (Neyland) in 1856, through trains called at Landore, from where a branch shuttle service connected with Swansea.

The through passenger services had expanded to eight trains each way by 1876, of which two were expresses, and one the 'mail'. In addition, there were five Vale of Neath services running through to Swansea over the main line. By this time, there was one up six-coach through train between Swansea (7.5 a.m.) and Paddington, whilst through Brake Composite coaches were connecting Swansea and Paddington in both directions, being attached to or detached from the Milford trains at Landore.

By the early 1880s, the through trains from London contained coaches for Tenby as well as for Milford and Swansea, and by the late 1890s for Pembroke Dock in place of Tenby.

Passenger locomotives working on London & West Wales services between Swindon and Neath in the mid-1890s were mainly '806/2201', 'Stella' and 'Barnum' class 2-4-0s based at those points. Westwards from Neath, 2-4-0s and 0-6-0 tender engines from Neath, Carmarthen and Milford were mainly utilised. On the Vale of Neath services to Swansea, '322', '1016', '1076' and '3571' class tanks were mostly to be seen.

From 1903, the schedules of engine working for London trains was altered, and locomotive changes were made at Cardiff, with

Port Talbot & Aberavon station, looking towards Cardiff. This posed photograph of the staff on the up platform was probably taken in the period after 1914, prior to which the Oakwood Mineral Railway still crossed the main line, where the level crossing was later to be sited. Port Talbot Middle box (formerly No.2) can be seen through the footbridge on the down (right) side, with the Up Main signal located at the end of the down platform for sighting purposes. The familiar stonework with block stone corners and lining is evident in the main buildings, a design used on the great majority of station and other structures in the area by the South Wales Railway. What was probably the Taibach Tinplate works can be seen in the distance on the right.
AUTHOR'S COLLECTION

4-4-0 classes of the 'Duke', 'Atbara', 'City' and 'Bulldog' becoming increasingly prominent.

A new form of passenger conveyance arrived during 1905 at Neath in the form of steam railmotors, which were introduced on the Vale of Neath services. These cars worked from Swansea East Dock over the route through Neath Low Level (Riverside) station, but did make an occasional appearance at the main line station en route to and from Neath shed. They survived at Neath until 1935.

The through services between Paddington and Neyland (renamed from New Milford in 1906) were continued by the GWR, whose trains also carried regular portions for Swansea (still detached/attached at Landore), Carmarthen and Pembroke Dock, with the occasional coach for Aberystwyth (via Carmarthen), providing an extremely good service between West Wales and London.

In 1906, a new loop line was opened to link High Street station directly with the Landore & Cockett line, with junctions at Loop East to the north of High Street, and Loop West on the Cockett line. This avoided the need for reversal at Landore, though for the first 20 years of its existence, the loop was only used by local services between High Street and West Wales; the London services and other through trains to the west continued to use the main line, with Swansea portions detached or attached at Landore as before, while the Fishguard boat trains ran through as complete formations.

Also in 1906, the Irish boat traffic was moved from New Milford to the newly-opened Fishguard Harbour station. The two daily Irish boat connections had only one-minute stops at Landore, emphasising the importance of their running times. In addition, until the start of the Great War, transatlantic liners en route from New York to Liverpool put in at Fishguard to provide a speedier transit to London. Connecting rail services were run for each liner arriving and these initially ran nonstop to Cardiff, where an engine change was made from two 4-4-0s to a London-based 'Star' Class, which then ran non-stop to Paddington. However, from May 1913 these services were accelerated by basing the 'Stars' at Fishguard and running the trains non-stop from there to Paddington, with

Fishguard-based train crew; this arrangement had been made possible by the installation of water troughs at strategic points along the route. The passage of the 'Fishguards' must have been very much the object of attention for the local railway enthusiasts of the time! Sadly, the onset of the 1914 War largely put an end to these services, the liners being vulnerable to U-boat attack, and eventually Fishguard was left with only the southern Irish boat traffic.

In 1913, the Swansea District line was opened to provide an alternative route to avoid Cockett bank. Essentially a freight line, it was also used by any passenger train which did not need to serve Swansea, for example the Fishguard & Paddington boat trains (including the transatlantic liner connections and return empty stock during the period up to 1914), excursions, some parcels and milk services, and empty stock.

The summer of 1914 is regarded by many as the zenith of Great Western train services. In that season, Swansea High Street had three main starting services to Paddington at 8.35, 11.40 a.m. and 3.35 p.m., with a balancing number of Swansea services in the down direction (10.50 a.m., 3.35 and 6.10 p.m. Paddington). There were another seven through trains in each direction to or from Fishguard or Neyland, calling at Landore. Again, most of these called only at Bridgend, Port Talbot and Neath en route to or from Landore or Swansea.

Although the great majority of South Wales traffic using the North & West route originated or terminated at Cardiff, a pair of vehicles were attached to the 2.45 p.m. Swansea to Pontypool Road train for Birkenhead and Birmingham, the latter running via Hereford and Worcester. By 1914, a Birmingham & Tenby portion had also become a regular summer feature in South Wales, the coaches being forwarded off the 8.0 a.m. Birmingham to Cardiff.

A gradual reduction of passenger services took place during the Great War, and by the end of 1917 there were just seven down and six up through services running, although troop and other military trains more than made up the deficit in numbers from the prewar era.

The postwar recovery was slow, due to the lack of manpower and materials, although by the summer of 1922 through services had

Swansea High Street station on 19th September 1926, as seen from The Refuge in Alexandra Road, before construction of the new facilities commenced. The end façade of the train shed is viewed here, with the end of the main station building block to its left. The sliding doors set in the end provided easy exit from the station platforms to the cab rank and the town, and were noted to be especially useful on Saturdays or on excursion days when the exits on the main buildings would prove to be inadequate in allowing the dispersal of large crowds.

WELSH INDUSTRIAL & MARITIME MUSEUM

Another view of Swansea High Street station, this time from Williams's faggot shop on High Street, 19th September 1926. The southern end of the main station buildings are seen in the centre of the view. After the rebuilding, this area was incorporated into a façade that curved around from the new structure on Ivey Place.
WELSH INDUSTRIAL & MARITIME MUSEUM

The main station buildings, situated off High Street (seen in the background) on 25th April 1933. The far section housed the parcels office, with separate inbound and outbound doors, whilst that to the left and beyond contained the booking hall and offices, cloak and waiting rooms, and other facilities. The Divisional offices were on the first floor. These views essentially illustrate the station erected in 1879.
WELSH INDUSTRIAL & MARITIME MUSEUM

The character of a bygone age is seen in this internal view of the train shed at High Street, looking across from the arrival side to the departure on 25th April 1933, showing the old timber platforms, with the main station buildings on platform No. 2 forming the background. The concertina-style sliding metal doors and solid timber doors at the ends of the platforms are both well illustrated in this view

WELSH INDUSTRIAL & MARITIME MUSEUM

Another internal view of the train shed at Swansea High Street, looking across the end circulating area. An enquiry office and confectionery kiosk are seen on the left, with the parcels office in the main station buildings beyond.	WELSH INDUSTRIAL & MARITIME MUSEUM

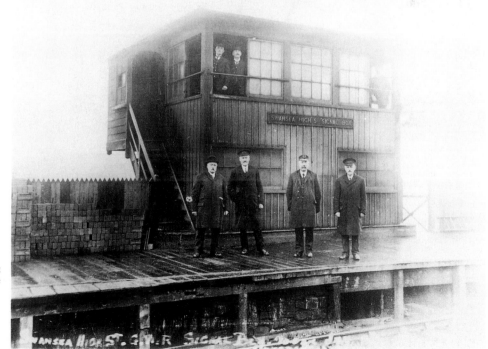

A portrait of Swansea High Street signal box in the early twentieth century, with the inevitable collection of staff in attendance.

The forecourt of Swansea High Street station in Ivey Place, probably taken in the early 1930s, and showing a little of the surrounding townscape. Station buildings were constructed in the attractive stonework design seen elsewhere along the line. The old platforms were replaced by much lengthened ones in 1926/7, but the new station buildings were not completed until the mid-1930s. The High Street runs diagonally across this picture.

GW TRUST

risen to nine in each direction. These included the three 'traditional' Swansea trains each way, with an additional up departure at 5.30 p.m., together with Neyland and Fishguard trains. The through coaches to Pembroke Dock and Aberystwyth were also in operation.

Also on the scene from July 1920 was the 'Ports-to-Ports' express, which ran daily between Swansea and Newcastle in each direction, with Great Central and Great Western trains on alternate days. This express had been introduced in May 1906 between Barry

and Newcastle, but upon its reintroduction after the Great War, it was extended westwards to Swansea. The up train left at 7.40 a.m., and the down arrived at 8.45 p.m., calling intermediately at Neath, Port Talbot, Bridgend, Barry, Penarth, Cardiff, Chepstow and Gloucester. The train ran via the Banbury & Cheltenham route, and joined the Great Central at Banbury for the journey to the north. Hull was also served by a through coach attached to this train. This service operated until the outbreak of the Second World War, with a Sunday train to and from Sheffield. Although this train

One of Landore's two '1076' class 0–6–0PTs – No. 1235 – entering Swansea High Street station with a late-morning auto service on Tuesday, 14th August 1934. This might have been the 10.35 a.m. from Port Talbot, due into High Street at 11.22 a.m., having run via the District line to Felin Fran and the Morriston branch thence. The '1076' or 'Buffalo' tanks were a large class of 266 engines, though after the numerous withdrawals of the late 1920s and early 30s, their numbers had been reduced to 90 by the beginning of 1934, with a further thirty going in that year. No. 1235 moved on from Landore in the following year, and was withdrawn in 1937.   C. B. L. WARWICK/ AUTHOR'S COLLECTION

Rebuilding work at High Street station, seen here in the early 1930s, looking north. The large train shed at the terminal end had been substantially removed, to be replaced by a covered concourse on the back of the new buildings on Ivey Place, with platform canopies extended to meet. The steelwork of old and new arrangements intermingle in this view.

L & GRP

The platforms at High Street, seen from platform No. 5 at a quiet moment in April 1939. The gentlemen's lavatories are seen on the right, at the end of the new eastern-side building, with staff and service offices between it and the refreshment rooms, running along to the right of the photographer. A screen wall continued beyond the building to the far end of the canopy.

NATIONAL RAILWAY MUSEUM

Swansea High Street station seen in April 1939, showing the new south fascia to Ivey Place executed in Portland stone. The main entrance led to the booking hall and office, with the hall concourse and the circulating area at the platform ends beyond. The external windows between the entrances and exits indicate the position of the booking office, whose booking windows faced the platforms, whilst the refreshment room was at the right-hand end of the fascia. The bus and a van were parked up against the arrivals side of the station. The cloakroom, parcels office, waiting rooms and lavatories were located on the sides of the station.

NATIONAL RAILWAY MUSEUM

was re-introduced in 1946, it was soon confined to weekend periods, and ceased entirely in 1961.

The vast majority of through coaches from and to the L & NWR via Shrewsbury terminated at Cardiff, but in 1922 pairs of coaches were running between Swansea, Manchester and Birkenhead in each direction.

Around this time, auto services commenced from Swansea, running via the Morriston branch to Felin Fran, Port Talbot and other destinations.

Principal passenger services at this time were mostly worked by 'Saints', with 'Stars' taking over from around 1932, followed on the main trains by 'Castles'. Only the 'Kings' and '47XXs' were not to be seen. 'Bulldogs' and '43XXs' were common on secondary and local trains, being joined by 'Halls' in the 1930s.

Following the lengthening of platforms at and the rebuilding of High Street station, from 1926 all services between London and Carmarthen or beyond, that had previously called only at Landore, now ran into and out of High Street station by means of the Swansea West Loop and the Landore & High Street routes. From this time, London services normally attached or detached their restaurant car portions at Swansea, where a strong complement of dining car staff were based.

At the same time, the express calls at Landore ceased, and that station came to lose some of its more advanced facilities, such as the refreshment room. The old 'shuttle services' that had plodded back-wards and forwards between the two stations since the 1850s were also withdrawn.

Another adjustment in 1926 was the inclusion of Milford Haven on the list of through coaches. Due to its proximity with Neyland, it was not usual to have through coaches to or from those two locations formed within the same train.

Fast train services to and from London remained around nine throughout the 1920s and 30s, though with occasional exceptions. Other through express services or coaches to and from Birmingham, Manchester, Liverpool and Birkenhead continued throughout this period, whilst a summer through train ran to and from Paignton. During the summer months, services to such destinations as Brighton and Weymouth were operated on Saturdays, with a combined train leaving High Street at 10.45 am., though with no direct return.

Some local trains ran between Cardiff and Swansea, others variously between Port Talbot, Neath and Swansea. In addition, the odd train ran to and from Bristol and Gloucester, either for parcels and mail purposes, or for linking with other services to and from Cardiff. Some stopping trains ran beyond Swansea, to Carmarthen or Neyland, as did several local trains from Swansea itself. By the late 1930s, Swansea auto cars were also to be found on main-line services, running out to Lando and Kidwelly, with diesel cars operating as far as Port Talbot and Whitland.

The amalgamation of the Vale of Neath company with the GWR in 1865 meant that services from Pontypool Road, Merthyr and Aberdare were now able to use High Street station, a position that largely continued until the closure of the VoN in 1965, though with far fewer services working through by that time. The Rhondda & Swansea Bay services from Treherbert used stations at Danygraig, Swansea East Dock and Swansea Riverside, but all these were closed in the mid-1930s with a few remaining services diverted into High Street.

Swansea possessed two other passenger termini in addition to High Street. The first was Swansea St. Thomas, situated in dockland territory, the terminus for Midland Railway services from Brynamman, Ystalyfera, Clydach and Pontardawe, and the Swansea Valley Line. The other was Swansea Victoria, where the L & NWR had set up their service from and to Shrewsbury by deftly acquiring the original companies that made up the route; these services were to last until 1964, when the line below Pontardulais into Victoria was closed and the Shrewsbury services diverted into Llanelly.

Wartime again saw a reduction in services, though this time the curtailment was immediate. In the depths of the conflict, there were an average of seven trains each way between London and Swansea, with Neyland and Pembroke Dock now the main destinations in the west, with Fishguard services much reduced.

By the early 1950s, the timetable had increased to ten daily express trains each way, with two to and from Fishguard once more, and Milford Haven back on the itinerary. The Aberystwyth through coaches of prewar days did not re-appear. More through services were developed on summer Saturdays, to avoid the need to change trains at Cardiff. The main services to West Wales from Swansea were mostly provided by Paddington services, though a few other trains from Cardiff and Bristol ran through, with supporting stopping services starting at Swansea for Llanelly, Pembrey and Carmarthen. Cardiff and Swansea local trains again provided the main stopping services to the east.

With a huge demand for line capacity by freight services, especially the developing oil traffic during the early 1960s, railway management decided that stopping passenger trains along the main line would be withdrawn, as their revenue yield was tiny in comparison with that from heavy freight. This led to the progressive closure of Pyle (and Porthcawl), Briton Ferry, Skewen, Llansamlet North and Landore stations during the mid-1960s.

The valuable and well-appreciated passenger service to West Wales was, however, costly in terms of coach utilisation, with many through coaches only doing a single trip in one direction, to or from Paddington, each day. Carmarthen and Swansea vehicles tended to be better utilised, as it was possible to get a double journey in some of the schedules within normal daytime workings.

In September 1963, through portion working on London services was withdrawn, with most Paddington trains terminating or starting at Swansea High Street, and a connecting service, sometimes a stopping train, serving stations beyond, though Fishguard Harbour services still ran through as complete trains. As services beyond Swansea became mostly DMU worked, this effectively saw the end of passenger steam working beyond Swansea. With the introduction of fixed-formation, High Speed trains in 1976, it soon became the norm to operate some trains at the start and end of the day through from/to Carmarthen.

FREIGHT TRAFFIC

In the early days, the line carried little goods, and it was not until 1853 that minerals were shown in the statistics.

By 1876, goods services amounted to some fifteen through in each direction, with a couple more working between Tondu and Port Talbot or Neath, plus some purely local movements. The goods trains included the Irish traffic to and from New Milford, and four or five minerals or empties. These services were predominantly hauled by the 0-6-0 varieties, both tender and tank.

The problems posed by Cockett bank for goods traffic and the need to provide more line accommodation through the Swansea area led to the opening of the Swansea District Line in 1913, between Court Sart Jct. (north of Briton Ferry) or Skewen East, and Morlais Junction on the line from Pontardulais to Llanelly. This route was primarily utilised for goods services, although a small number of passenger and passenger-rated trains that did not serve Swansea also ran over it. Various industrial concerns were served off the line, including Llandarcy oil refinery, and several collieries.

Whilst the South Wales Railway mainly came to the area for passenger service purposes, strongly encouraged by the GWR in its pursuit of a through passenger service to Ireland, all other railway companies local to South Wales had sought access from the beginning to the lucrative coal traffic between colliery and dock, plus the conveyance of iron, copper, limestone, etc., used in early iron smelting – all part of the Industrial Revolution that spread throughout South Wales. Whilst all the smaller companies developed an element of passenger service, either at their own volition or under pressure from local communities, each of them was primarily in existence for the freight traffic. All conveyed coal traffic to the docks at Swansea, Neath or Briton Ferry, the latter two being more wharves than docks.

The continually-expanding Swansea Docks was the object of attention for the Great Western, Midland and L & NW companies there, with the developing amounts of general cargo import and export traffic eagerly pursued. The export coal was mostly in the hands of the GWR, who ran direct services to the docks from many of the collieries and yards in the surrounding area, from the Neath & Brecon line in the east to the Burry Port & Gwendraeth Valley line in the west.

With each concern having its own sidings and yards in the various areas of operation, all combined to produce an intricate pattern of railways with a high demand for shunting and tripping.

The through goods scene by 1914 had expanded to around thirty trains in each direction, together with a number of local workings. The first of the new, fast vacuum services had appeared by this time, with two Fishguard trains in each direction hauled by 4-4-0s to the west of Cardiff. Perishable and other faster goods trains were also often worked by 4-4-0s. Although the majority of ordinary services were still worked by 0-6-0s, some '28XX' 2-8-0s were now to be seen on Llanelly and Severn Tunnel Jct. trains, '26XX' 2-6-0s from Tondu and Neath, and 2-8-0Ts from Neath and Llanelly.

In the 1930s freight operations, virtually every Great Western class of tender and large tank could be seen, with a vast array of the old 0-6-0 tank engines on local and shunting turns, being gradually replaced in the expansion of the '57XXs' from the 1930s. 'Halls' and 'Granges' appeared on the vacuum services, but the '47XX' 2-8-0s were not permitted to run into Wales.

Between Bridgend and Swansea, there were significant industrial installations at Steel Company of Wales, Margam; Port Talbot Steelworks and Docks; Briton Ferry Steelworks and Docks; and Neath Metal Box, to name but a few. The area to the north of Swansea also contained major industrial concerns. In addition, each town had its own goods sundries depot and full-load yards, each generating its own level of servicing, with nests of sidings at each for putting together trains for onward main-line conveyance, or receiving and breaking down trains from yards further east, such as Severn Tunnel Junction, Newport and Cardiff.

By the mid-1950s, freight traffic had grown to a considerable level, with around sixty movements of through traffic in each direction. Much of the down traffic terminated within the area under consideration at Margam (Briton Ferry), Swansea East Dock, Felin Fran, Landore Steel Works, Landore, and the yards at Swansea (High Street). Of those heavy freight services running through, most terminated around Llandilo Jct. and Llanelly, whilst vacuum trains were destined for Llandilo Jct, Llanelly, Carmarthen, Whitland and Fishguard. By far the greatest amount of the heavier traffic originated at yards within South Wales itself, particularly from those at and around Severn Tunnel Jct., Newport and Cardiff. In addition to all these were the local and trip workings.

For an area of such intense freight activity, there was for many years a need for a central marshalling yard; this was only provided as late as 1960 with the opening of Margam Yard (qv), which enabled far greater discipline to be injected into freight working in the area. Prior to this, the best marshalling facilities probably existed at Swansea East Dock, where many main-line services started and terminated; at Llandilo Junction, Llanelly; and at Jersey Marine, for colliery services.

The great majority of coal traffic for the two major concerns in the area, SCOW (later BSC) Margam coking coal for the making of steel, and Swansea Docks for shipment, was conveyed in through block trains from colliery to consumer and therefore did not need yard access en route (other than that coming off the BP & GV). Other than this, most of the freight traffic of the 1950s required access to marshalling facilities, but with the arrival of the 1960s, a new business in the form of oil traffic 'exploded' in West Wales, with refineries being set up at Milford Haven and Pwllcrochan, producing through fully-fitted trains of 100-ton oil tanks running at Class 6 (the highest freight category). This added to the traffic to and from the older refinery at Llandarcy, Swansea, which mostly produced 'wagon load' traffic, but soon joined the block train scene. Several of the leading oil companies were involved: Shell, BP, Esso, Texaco and Amoco each imposed tight demands on the railway for quality transits to consumers in England.

In addition, new traffics such as liquefied petroleum gas came into being, just one of a number of new commodities now being consigned by rail from this area. In addition, anthracite assumed a far greater demand in the smokeless zones of London and the Home Counties, producing through trains of hoppers direct to Coal Concentration Depots, running at class 7 with a good vacuum head of new fitted wagons.

Rationalisation of goods facilities was widespread during the latter half of the 1960s, with house coal (often the major traffic at small station yards) concentrated at larger depots, goods sundries depots closed and full load handling removed, enabling such traffic to be dealt with at the larger remaining depots, which ultimately became Swansea only.

The removal of vast numbers of sidings and connections from the line enabled Multiple Aspect Signalling to be introduced at signifi-cantly lower cost than would otherwise have been the case, and 1963 saw a new MAS box introduced at Port Talbot covering the entire area of the main line from Cardiff Panel in the east.

MOTIVE POWER DEPOTS

On the motive power scene in the 1950s/60s, there were three main-line depots between Bridgend and Swansea: Duffryn Yard (a former Port Talbot Railway shed), Neath and Landore. The main depot was at Neath, the motive power area being the Neath Division, covering all depots between Port Talbot and West Wales, and including the local depots of Danygraig and Swansea East Dock, former R & SB and Swansea Harbour Trust depots housing the docks shunting and tripping engines, the original passenger engines of the R & SB, and some main-line large tank freight engines.

The depots at Duffryn Yard and Neath were essentially freight depots, with many shunting and tripping tank engines allocated. Duffryn Yard also housed a fleet of large tanks, while for much of the time, Neath had a modest fleet of 2-8-0 and 2-6-0 engines for main-line freight purposes as well as the usual large tank designs. There were some local passenger duties at both depots, including along the Vale of Neath to Pontypool Road, worked latterly by '41XX' and '56XX' class engines from Neath, and R & SB services to Treherbert.

The main passenger depot was at Landore which housed a fleet of 'Castle' class engines for working to Paddington, Cardiff and West Wales. From about 1930 until the early 1950s, the depot had a large fleet of 'Star' class 4-6-0s which originally worked to London but were progressively replaced by 'Castles'. In the late 1950s and early 60s, the depot acquired a glowing reputation for the presentation of its 'Castles' on the London services, with silver-painted buffers, a feature introduced by shedmaster Roy White, to enable Landore crews to recognise their engines at foreign sheds. Though these are now but a fond memory, one of the stalwart Landore 'Castles' remains in preservation at Didcot – No. 5051 *Earl Bathurst* which was regularly to be seen hauling the 'Pembroke Coast Express' and the 'South Wales Pullman'.

Progressively from 1961–65, diesel traction took over from steam throughout the area, with a wholesale reduction in the number of engine sheds required. Together with the closure of signal boxes, stations and station yards, sidings and small marshalling yards, the scene between Bridgend and Swansea now bears little resemblance to what it was when the photographs illustrating each place along the line in this volume were taken. Though passenger speeds have increased considerably, much of the general freight once conveyed by rail from Swansea Docks and the steel and tinplate works in the area, now passes along the M4 Motorway en route to distant locations. One wonders whether overall this has been the progress it should have been, when the SWML stands empty for long periods while the motorway traffic increases every day.

A westbound five-coach local, with a van at the rear, standing alongside the down platform, Bridgend, behind Canton 'Saint' No. 2940 *Dorney Court* in the early 1950s. This engine was condemned in January 1952. The Valleys platform is seen to the far left, serving the Llynvi, Ogmore and Garw branches via Tondu. In the early 1950s, most of these ran to Abergwynfi, with a few to Nantymoel or Blaengarw. The branches were also served by passenger or workmen's trains running intermediately from Tondu or Brynmenyn Jct. A few branch trains from Bridgend ran only as far as Tondu.   R. C. RILEY

STORMY DOWN

Four miles west of Bridgend was Stormy Down, approached by a westbound three-mile climb of between 1 in 132 and 1 in 163. However, it was in the eastbound direction that the biggest problems were encountered, with a maximum gradient of 1 in 93 between Pyle and Stormy summit, which required heavy freight trains to be banked from Margam Moors. From here, the gradient rose at 1 in 139, but approaching Pyle steepened with short sections at 1 in 102, 94 and 79 before settling at 1 in 93 through Pyle for the 1¼ miles to the summit.

A map of the area in 1881 shows a siding on the up side and two on the down, the latter by 1904 serving B. Daniel Jones & Company's limeworks, with a trailing crossover between the main lines, all adjacent to Stormy Sidings signal box at 194m. 51ch. In 1908, the up goods refuge siding was rated for 59 wagons, engine & van.

In 1912, the box was renewed and the three sidings extended into loops, with capacities of 67 (No. 1 Down), 65 (No. 2 Down) and 67 (Up) wagons, in addition to the engine & van. Connections

were added at the east end out of the down main, and were later extended at the west end.

Stormy was to have been the site of a large marshalling yard of around thirty sidings in a memorandum published in 1920, with a new down goods loop running from Bridgend, and an up loop from Margam Moors. The construction of yards for traffic for and from West Wales was considered 'here, or elsewhere in the neighbourhood of Margam', though Stormy would have the advantage of 'natural gradients'. The plan for Stormy was abandoned shortly afterwards.

In 1931, the sidings are shown in the use of Stormy Products Co., and in 1937 passed to Welsh Refractories Ltd., finally ending with N.B. Allen and South Wales Refractories from 1939.

The southernmost siding was taken out of service in 1964, leaving single loops on the down and up sides. Under the MAS scheme of September 1965, the box and the up and down loops were all removed, leaving only plain track.

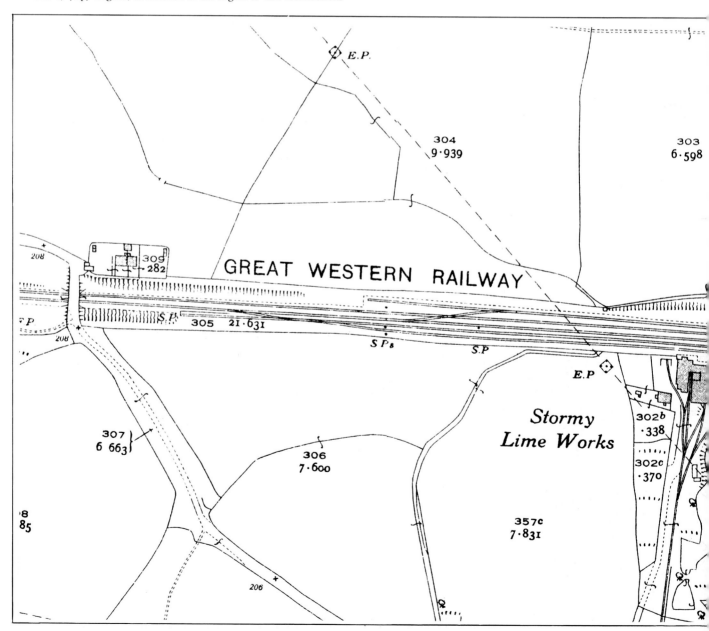

A 'Hall' on the down 'Pembroke Coast Express', the fastest service on the South Wales main line, was a rarity indeed, but Landore's No. 5913 *Rushton Hall* had only come on at Cardiff to replace the ailing Landore 'Castle' No. 7028, on Easter Monday, 2nd April 1956. The 10.55 a.m. Paddington train is seen at speed, starting the 1 in 93 descent on the upper section of Stormy bank, running non-stop between Cardiff and Swansea. The 8-coach load was well within the Hall's capabilities; between those two places with this service, the limiting load for a '49XX' was 392 tons, some twelve or thirteen coaches. The old refractory site can be seen on the right, and though there is no evidence of traffic in the sidings, the private siding agreement was not legally terminated until 1965. Stormy Sidings box can be seen beyond the last coach.   R. O. TUCK

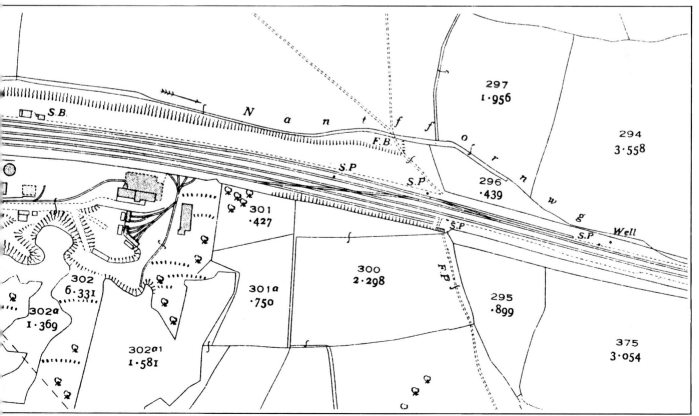

Taken from 25-inch Ordnance Survey for 1940. (Crown copyright reserved)

An up class 'H' freight, formed mostly of wagons of anthracite, seen climbing Stormy bank on 14th March 1962 behind a hard-working '42XX', possibly Canton's No. 5225, banked in the rear by an 0–6–0PT. The engine had passed the Stormy box Up Distant, well into the 1 in 93 section of the bank. The '42XXs' could take 42 loaded (10-ton) mineral wagons up the steepest gradient between Pyle and Stormy, but this was increased by 26 with a group 'C' pannier tank assisting.

R. O. TUCK

The rear of the same train, viewed from the same location as the train passed, showing the pannier assisting the '42XX'. The 4-mile bank from Margam Moors to Stormy Sidings in the up direction climbed initially at a gradient of 1 in 139, but then tightened to 1 in 93 for the final 1¼ miles, for which banking power was necessary for many freights The train had about 38 wagons, but many of these were greater than the 'standard' 10-ton mark, and would have been counted as more than one wagon for engine haulage purposes. The train engine was approaching the bridge to the west of Stormy box, which can just be seen under the span.   R. O.TUCK

The 12.40 p.m. Carmarthen to Cheltenham approaching the top of Stormy bank on 2nd April 1956 behind Gloucester 'Mogul' No. 6381, with a longer train than usual, doubtless reflecting additional traffic on this Easter Monday. This service was scheduled for a 4-coach corridor set, one of five that worked a 5-day cycle variously between Newport, Swansea, Pontypool Road, Carmarthen, Cheltenham, Cardiff, Shrewsbury, Hereford, Porthcawl and Newport. The fish van behind the engine was running from Milford Haven to Salisbury, and would be attached to the 4.25 p.m. Portsmouth train at Cardiff. On this day, the train was handed over at Cardiff to Canton 'Standard Class 4' No. 75021, which worked on to Gloucester, departing Cardiff at 3.42 p.m.   R. O.TUCK

PYLE

The original 1850s main-line station at Pyle was located a quarter-of-a-mile to the west of the later junction station, in the centre of what eventually became the top side of the inverted triangle formed with the two Porthcawl branch access lines.

Until 1876, the Llynfi & Ogmore Railway line to Porthcawl was independent of the GWR route at Pyle, and had its own single-line station alongside the main road to Cardiff. However, in 1876 the two were linked together by a line between Pyle No. 1 signal box (opened to control the east end of the link line, at the junction with the L & O), and Pyle No.2 (at the west end, on the GWR line). The 'No. 2' box existed before this time, to control access to sidings on the north side of the GWR line.

In 1882, the L & O line to Porthcawl was re-aligned, the former trackbed being abandoned and a new line constructed closer to the GWR, partly along the link line between the L & O and the GWR, together with two loop sidings on its north side. A new

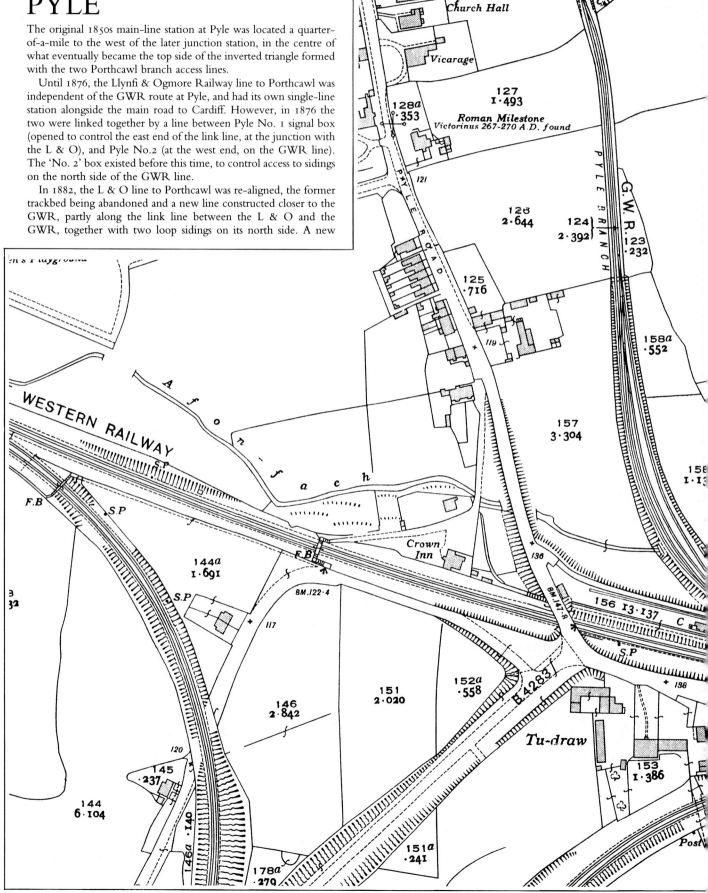

The east end of Pyle station in 1955, with the 8.55 a.m. Paddington to West Wales service (No. 163) passing East box behind a returning Landore 'Castle'. At this time, the first four vehicles behind the engine (including the dining car, third in the formation) came off at Swansea (High Street), whist five for Pembroke Dock and three for Neyland (order reversed from Swansea) continued onwards.   S. RICKARD

L & O station was built just to the south of No. 2 signal box, but as yet the GWR station remained a quarter of a mile further west.

The L & O was amalgamated with the Great Western in July 1883. In 1886, a new station with staggered platforms was built opposite the former L & O station, and then the old South Wales Railway station was closed. The new station formed a narrow 'V' shape as the Porthcawl and main lines diverged to the west.

A branch (the 'Pyle Branch') was opened in 1898 from Waterhall Junction, on the Ogmore Vale Extension line between Tondu and Margam, to the yard on the north side of the line. The former No. 2 signal box was rebuilt in 1900 and became 'Pyle Junction'. By this time there were two separate double junction complexes between the main and branch routes, one serving each direction, with the new Junction box between them.

In 1912, the former L & O line through the station was doubled, and a new down platform provided. At the same time, the GWR down platform was extended eastwards to join with the up branch platform, which was similarly extended, forming a 'V' shaped site.

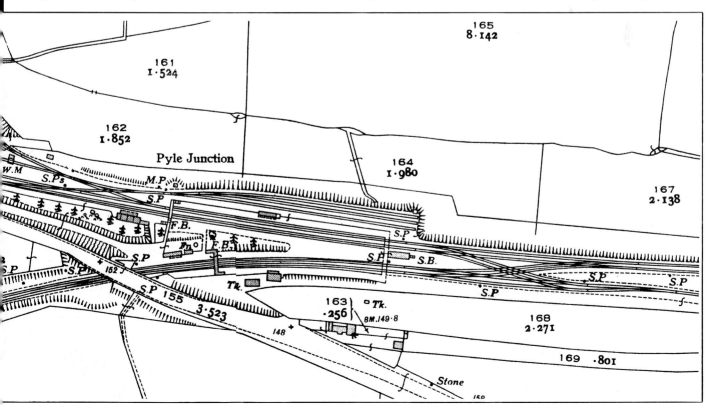

Taken from 25-inch Ordnance Survey for 1942. (Crown copyright reserved)

A new 'double scissors' crossover was provided to the east of the Junction box at Pyle station to replace the two separate complexes, the site of the westerly one having being absorbed by the platform lengthenings.

Doubling of the Porthcawl line beyond Pyle station to Cornelly was carried out in 1924.

In 1947, the Pyle West Curve was opened to provide a direct link with Porthcawl from the Swansea direction, and Pyle West Junction opened in March of that year, initially for freight traffic, with a summer Sundays passenger service from Swansea. From 1949, a twice-daily passenger service from Swansea operated, worked by Landore diesel railcars, though in 1953 one of the trips was made by an auto, and the second Saturday trip by a conventional train. By 1957, all trips were worked by engine and coaches, providing a greater carrying capacity, which was particularly required on summer weekends. Pyle West Curve closed on 1st February 1965, and the box in the following September with the introduction of MAS.

The Pyle area was decimated by the MAS alterations in 1965. By then, the Waterhall branch coming in from the north had been closed, as had passenger services on the Porthcawl branch, and in that year the Porthcawl branch was closed to the remaining goods traffic. Nearly all the surviving crossovers and sidings were removed, though a trailing connection remained from the branch to the down main for a few years more. Now, only plain track exists where once there had been a considerable railway presence.

A view looking east from the end of the down main platform at Pyle on 28th July 1963, showing the end of the East box, the bracket Up Starting signals at the end of both platforms for the main and Tondu routes, and the water column on the up branch. The end of the stop block of the nearest of the three dead-end sidings that ran behind the Up Main platform can just be seen to the left of the up main signal, these being served from the Waterhall branch end.
P. J. GARLAND

The main-line platforms at Pyle, looking east in the autumn of 1963, with a view of the stone-built waiting rooms on the up side. The reference to the Porthcawl branch had been removed from the station nameboards following closure of the branch to passengers on 9th September 1963.

LENS OF SUTTON COLLECTION

A panoramic view of the east end of Pyle station taken on 28th July 1963 from the footbridge on the Porthcawl Branch platforms. The single-line branch from Tondu crossed underneath the main line about three-quarters-of-a-mile to the east of Pyle station, then swung westwards to eventually run alongside it for a short distance through the site en route to Porthcawl; the branch can be seen entering the station from the right of centre, with the main line to the left, connected by double junctions beyond Pyle East (formerly Junction) signal box. A large water tower stood behind the Down Branch platform, seen here on the right.
P. J. GARLAND

Pyle East signal box at the east end of the island platform on 28th July 1963. The waiting room and toilet block on the Up Main platform can be seen to the left of the box, with the open footbridge between the main platforms beyond. Wagons can just be seen on the sidings behind the Up Main platform.
P. J. GARLAND

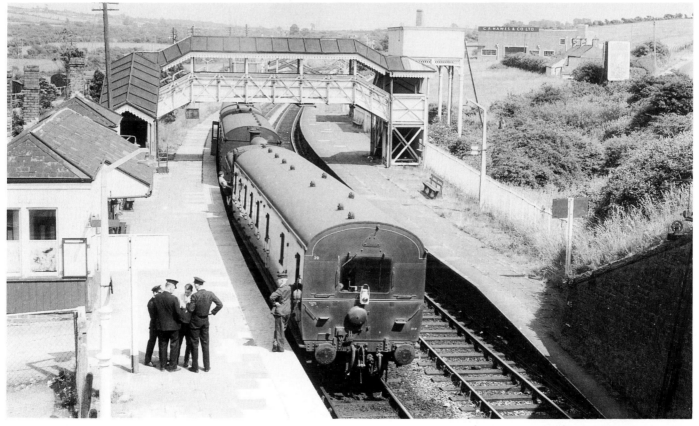

Another view along the Porthcawl branch platform at Pyle, with Tondu's '64XX' 0–6–0PT No.6431 sandwiched in a 3-coach auto on 7th July 1962, with more staff than passengers visible. By this time, nearly all of the auto services ran just between Pyle and Porthcawl, with empty workings to and from Tondu, though one afternoon return auto journey from Porthcawl to Tondu was carried out daily.
S. RICKARD

The west end of the Porthcawl branch platforms terminated against the buttresses of the road bridge carrying the main A48 Cardiff & Carmarthen road, with the up branch platform buildings on the right. Both platforms were signalled for use in the down direction, those trains from the up side joining the down branch by the crossover beyond the road bridge. The branch was double track for the 1½ miles between Pyle station and Cornelly. 28th July 1963.
P.J. GARLAND

A view of '4400' Class 2–6–2T No. 4404 at the Up Branch platform on 10th September 1951, the picture taken from under the A48 roadbridge which spanned the branch tracks at their west end. '44s' had been at Tondu since 1908, with one engine No. 3106 (4406 from the December 1912 renumbering) from November of that year, joined by No. 115 (No.4400) in May 1912. The class was absent from the area during 1924–31, but thereafter two engines were again allocated.   H. C. CASSERLEY

Pyle Station, looking east on 17th June 1959, with Tondu's '45XX' 2–6–2T No. 5534 standing at the Up Branch platform with an auto service from Porthcawl; fifteen of the '4575' series were fitted with auto gear in 1953 for service in the Cardiff and Bridgend districts. In the summer months, the branch platforms saw through trains from and to Newport, Cardiff and Bridgend, as well as excursions from further afield. Little traffic can be seen on the A48 road, to the right.　　STATIONS UK

The larger '51XX' 2–6–2T worked through services from Newport and Cardiff to Porthcawl, and here Tondu's No. 4121 is seen alongside the down branch platform on 14th July 1959 with empty stock for Porthcawl, which would return with a hefty load of day trippers. The class appeared at Tondu in 1946.　H. C. CASSERLEY

'56XX' 0–6–2T No. 5670 alongside the Down Branch platform with a van in September 1963. By the late 1950s, most freight seen through the branch platforms was for Cornelly, although a Tondu, Porthcawl & Margam trip was also operating. A daily afternoon Tondu and Stormy duty also used the branch platforms. Tondu freight services over the branch from the 1930s were mostly worked by 'Bulldogs' and '2721' classes, and later by '56XXs' and '57XXs'.　　ROGER HOLMES

Pyle station in the autumn of 1963, looking west along the main line. The bridge carrying the A48 Cardiff & Carmarthen road can be seen in the distance, with the station's modest loading bank, goods lock-up and cattle pens to its right. To their right can be seen the single-line branch to Waterhall Jct., where it joined the Tondu & Margam (Ogmore Vale Extension) line. Also apparent in the yard are the connections to the three dead-end sidings that ran behind the Up Main platform.

LENS OF SUTTON COLLECTION

Another view looking west from the Down Main platform towards the A48 roadbridge and the compact goods yard. The footbridge at the site of the first Pyle main line station can be seen through the archway. Duffryn Yard's 0-6-0PT No. 9444, which had just serviced the yard, was returning home with the signal off for the down main line. 13th September 1952.

H. C. CASSERLEY

The 10.35 a.m. Kensington to Whitland Milk Empties behind a high-mileage Canton 'Hall' No. 6936 *Breccles Hall* heading into the evening sun through Pyle on 14th July 1959. From Cardiff, this train was sandwiched between the 3.45 p.m. and 3.55 p.m. Paddington to Fishguard trains as far as Court Sart, where it diverted off the main line to run via the Swansea District line. R. M. CASSERLEY

Having just passed Pyle West Junction, where the later line from the west to Porthcawl diverged from the main line, Bath Road Castle' No. 5000 *Launceston Castle* is seen with the 8.0 a.m. Neyland to Paddington service on Monday, 4th July 1955. The train was scheduled to convey four coaches from Swansea at the head, followed by four each from Neyland and Fishguard. Rather than the usual kitchen and dining cars found on South Wales trains, the leading portion incorporated a Kitchen Buffet Car. At this time, the 8.0 Neyland was worked between Swansea (10.30 a.m.) and Cardiff by a Bath Road high-mileage 'Castle' off the 5.50 a.m. Bristol to Cardiff and the 7.50 a.m. Cardiff to Swansea. At Cardiff, the engine on the 8.0 Neyland gave way to a Canton 'Britannia' or 'Castle' for the 12 noon departure to Paddington. The Bath Road 'Castle' later returned home with the 5.25 p.m. Cardiff to Bristol. S. RICKARD

Running between Pyle West Junction and Pyle station, the crews of up freight trains would have been building up the fire and gathering speed as they approached the 1 in 93 gradient from Pyle to Stormy Sidings. Ebbw Jct.'s 2–8–0 No. 3824 was working hard around the gentle bend from Pyle West Junction with an eastbound Class 'H' freight on 7th April 1955, still consisting mainly of wooden wagons.
S. RICKARD

With a clear road ahead, Canton '42XX' 2–8–0T No. 4266, still with inside steam pipes, should have had little trouble on Stormy Bank with this short train of empty steel carriers, probably bound for Cardiff (Guest, Keens) to pick up a load. Although coal traffic was much in evidence on this section, the preponderance of steel and metal works to the west also brought many such specialist vehicles into the section.
S. RICKARD

Enjoying the benefit of the short 1 in 79 section on the descent through Pyle, '52XX' No. 5201 from Ebbw Jct. shed is seen here coasting down between Pyle and Pyle West Junction on 4th July 1955 with a westbound class 'H' mixed freight, which included returning empty tinplate vans as 5th to 8th vehicles. The brake van of the train was still under the A48 road bridge, whilst the middle of the train was passing under a footbridge at the site of the first Pyle station, closed in 1886.

S. RICKARD

On 4th July 1955, Cathays-based '56XX' No. 6684 climbing through Pyle West Junction, in preparation for the sustained 1 in 93 gradient up Stormy bank with a return train of empty minerals from Margam to the Cardiff Valleys, the return working of the 10.15 a.m. Crockherbtown to Margam. Again the train is seen between Pyle West Junction and Pyle, passing the West box's advanced starter, which also carried Pyle East box's distant.

S. RICKARD

Western Valley coal for the Steel Company of Wales, Margam, was being conveyed by this Rogerstone to Margam coal train hauled by Ebbw Jct's 2–8–0T No. 4246, seen passing Pyle West box on a sunny Thursday, 5th January 1956. Pyle West Curve can be seen to the right of the train, paralleling the main line for a short distance before swinging right to meet up with the branch line from the station at Hoel y Sheet Crossing. This line opened in March 1947, and initially provided a direct path for freight trains between Margam and Porthcawl, and soon afterwards for a couple of diesel car workings from Swansea. In the later 1950s and early 60s, '41XXs' and '51XXs' operated these services, with trains of between three and eight coaches scheduled.

S. RICKARD

Llanelly '42XX' No. 5261 hauling a long load of apparently empty opens out of Pyle West Junction on 4th July 1955, with Stormy bank looming. On the bank, the '42s' could haul 84 empty wagons unassisted. The Cardiff Division created considerable numbers of empty opens, which were sent off to a pre-determined destination through Rolling Stock Office channels, probably outside the division for re-loading.

S. RICKARD

On 5th January 1956, Old Oak Common 'Castle' No. 7010 *Avondale Castle* recovering from a signal check on the approach to Pyle West Junction with a down train of milk empties, bound for Whitland. This train may have been a late-running overnight empties, possibly the 1.15 a.m. from Marston Sidings, as the regular daytime train – the 10.35 a.m. Kensington – was not due until well after sunset at this time of the year. The West Curve tracks are in the foreground, leading off to Porthcawl.

S. RICKARD

Drifting down the bank from Pyle station to Pyle West Junction on 5th January 1956, and passing the site of the old station, Llantrisant 2–8–0T No. 4208 was heading west with a train of coal from the Llantrisant Valleys, running as Class 'H'. The train could either have been the 9.30 a.m. Llantrisant to Llandilo Jct., a '42XX' duty, which would call at Margam, Briton Ferry, Felin Fran and Bynea en route, or a block load for SCOW, Margam.

S. RICKARD

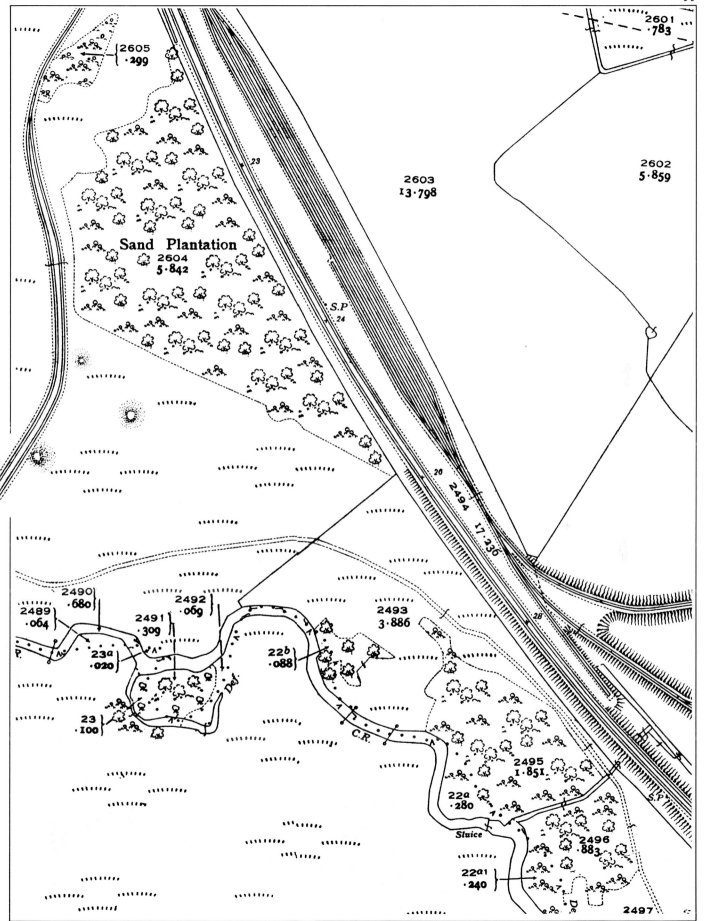

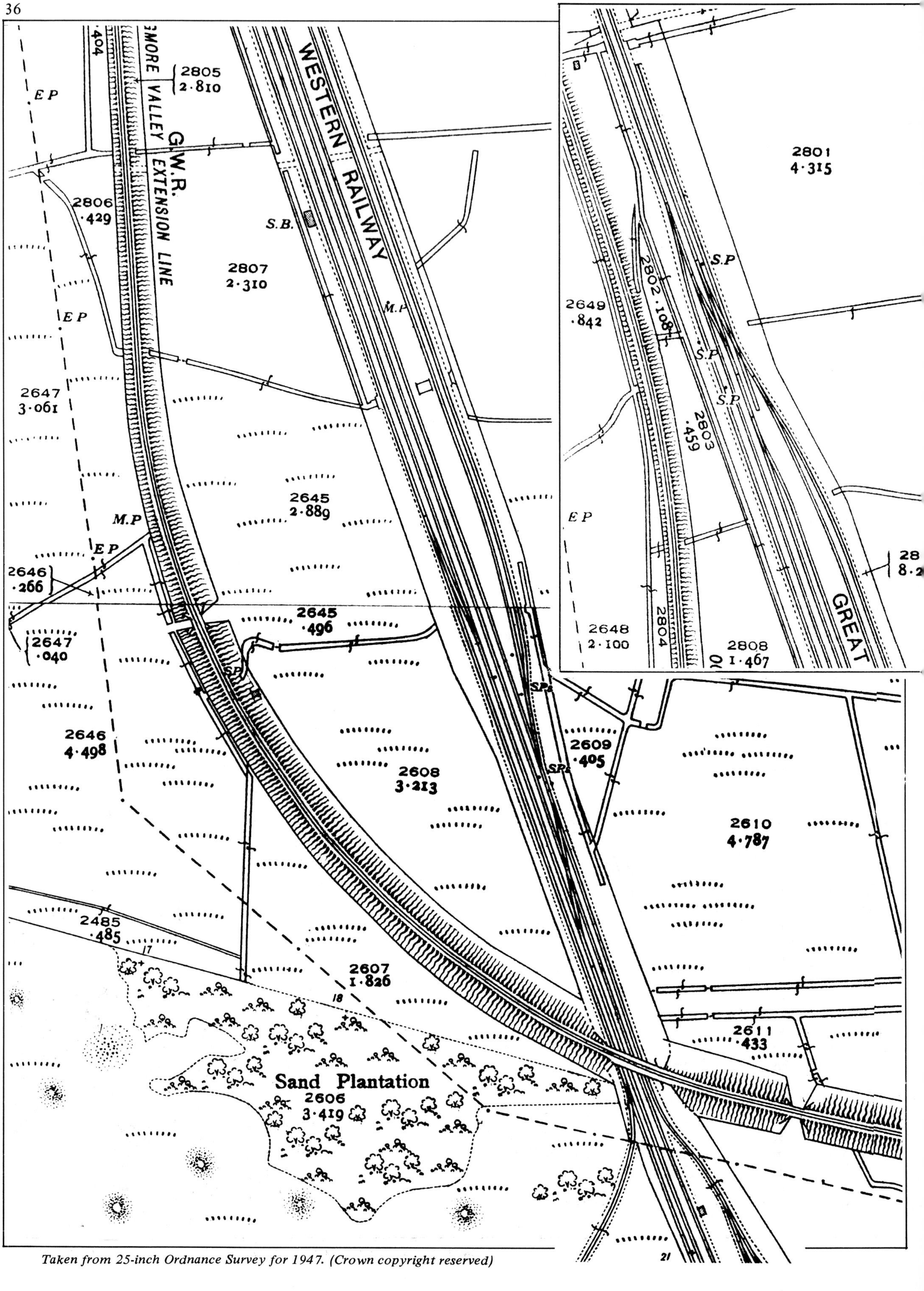

WESTERN RAILWAY

GREAT

G.W.R. EXTENSION LINE

...MORE VALLEY

.404

E P

2805
2·810

2806
·429

E P

2807
2·310

S.B.

M.P

2647
3·061

E P

2645
2·889

M.P

E P

2646
·266

2645
·496

2647
·040

S.P.

2646
4·498

2608
3·213

S.P.

2609
·405

S.P.

2610
4·787

2485
·485

17

18

2607
1·826

Sand Plantation
2606
3·419

2611
·433

2801
4·315

S.P

2802 ·108

S.P.

2649
·842

S.P.

2803
·459

E P

2648
2·100

2804

2808
1·467

28
8·2

21

MARGAM

MARGAM MARSHALLING YARD

Occupying an area of 170 acres, and comprising over 33 miles of plain track with 240 points and crossings, Margam Yard was officially opened on 11th April 1960, having been operational since 6th March. Built on Margam Moors, it was then the most highly-mechanised yard in the country.

The case for constructing the yard at such a late date in the history of railway freight operations lay in the huge amount of traffic passing to and from the Steel Company of Wales, Margam, to which the yard was adjacent; the expansion of the National Coal Board anthracite traffic from collieries in the Neath, Swansea and Llanelly Valleys; and the cramped marshalling facilities then existing for traffic to and from Swansea. There was also a need to cater for the growing number of fast freight services which needed to attach portions in the area, such as the block trains of anthracite to coal concentration depots in London and the Home Counties. There was already a small yard – Margam Down Sidings – consisting of 17 tracks, which by the late 1950s had become inadequate for the expanding traffic levels, and the construction of the new yard enabled this area to be handed over to SCOW for their own purposes.

Margam Yard was constructed on two-way principles, representing the traffic flows from east and west of Port Talbot. It was estimated that some 4,000 wagons per day would be dealt with at the yard, but a considerable margin for expansion was allowed for over this number. As with the main line in this area, the yard was generally aligned north-south.

At the south (up) end of the yard – which was accessed via Water Street Jct. signal box – were twelve Reception Sidings, all being accessible by traffic arriving from the east, and five from the west. There were four additional tracks through the reception sidings, with avoiding lines for arriving and departing traffic on the west and east sides of the yard respectively, whilst an Engine Release Road and a Hump Return Road were also provided. The avoiding line to the west of the complex was used especially for coal services for SCOW from pits in the Eastern & Western and Cardiff Valleys, which operated as fully-fitted block trains introduced progressively from 1960 onwards, running direct from colliery to consumer, the first being from Hafodyrynys Colliery in the Eastern Valley. The east side avoiding line was similarly used by returning block trains of empties, again running as fully-fitted trains direct to the colliery. Coal services from the Bridgend Valleys for SCOW, from the major supplying collieries in the Llynfi, Garw and Ogmore Valleys (Maesteg, Garw, Ffaldau, Rhondda Main etc), ran via the Ogmore Vale Extension Line, which crossed the main line on an overbridge and entered the Margam complex between the yard and the sorting sidings to its north, with direct access into the SCOW coal traffic holding sidings.

As traffic passed over the hump at the north end of the Reception Sidings, it was directed into one of the 51 sorting sidings under the guidance of the control tower at the south-western corner of the yard, the requirements for each train in the Reception Sidings having been passed electronically to the control tower in the form of a cut list, representing the number of wagons to be directed into each road for ongoing locations. Rafts of wagons for individual destinations were then drawn forward from the sorting sidings into the Secondary Sorting Sidings to the north of the Hump Yard for forming up in readiness for departure, the shunting necessary comprising the marshalling order in the train, vacuum head formation, etc.

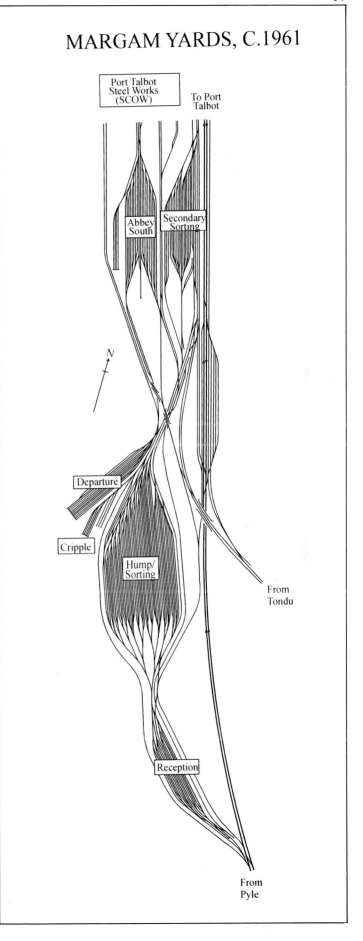

MARGAM YARDS, C.1961

Just to the north-west of the hump sorting sidings was a group of five Cripple Sidings with a covered area for major work, and a tranship platform and sidings where loads could be removed from defective wagons and placed on fresh ones. A buffer of eleven Holding Sidings was provided alongside the cripple sidings, used for holding excess wagons on hand or for accommodating trains waiting departure in order to clear the Reception and Secondary Sorting Sidings.

An important requirement of the yard was to provide facilities for speedy portion working, whereby trains could attach traffic and be away quickly without having to enter the yard complex itself. This was carried out in a new Knuckle Yard, alongside the main line at the north end of the complex. Typical of this type of traffic were the coal concentration trains, which may have started at Llandilo Junction Yard, Llanelly, with a dozen or so loaded hoppers from Cynheidre Colliery, and would need to call at Margam to attach a further portion from Onllwyn/Banwen, conveying a through load of anthracite to one of the newly-introduced receiving depots in the London and Home Counties area, such as West Drayton, Watford, Chessington, etc. Other part loads may well have been received from Trostre/Velindre Tinplate Works, which required to be made up with other block loads for a speedier through transit.

Motive power for services from the yard was initially provided by Duffryn Yard and Neath steam depots, in addition to returning engines from other depots, but within a year of opening, diesel traction had begun to appear on South Wales freight in the form of the highly successful Class '37s', and a new diesel depot was opened on the north-eastern side of the Hump Sorting Sidings, following which the steam depots in the area were gradually phased out, with all steam activity ending by the end of 1965.

Though the yard fulfilled an urgent need at its opening, providing for the massive level of freight traffic passing to and from the Port Talbot, Neath, Swansea and Llanelly industrial areas (in addition to the considerable level of traffic for rural use in West Wales, such as cattle feed) within ten years, the amount had begun to decline substantially, and wagons of railway scrap became all too common. The Railways Board decision to withdraw from goods sundries ('smalls') traffic in 1972 removed a swathe of fitted wagons from the scene at a stroke, and this was followed by the withdrawal from 'wagon-load' traffic in 1976, itself designed to kill the need for marshalling yards on the system. This effectively created an increasing need for motorways, to carry this former railborne traffic by road. In addition, the rapid onset of the demise of the South Wales' coal industry, and a switch to imported coal, conspired to create a situation in which the South Wales Main Line yards at Severn Tunnel and Margam became increasingly superfluous.

In May 1979, eighteen of the hump sidings were disconnected from the hump; in August 1980, the use of the hump facility ceased, the retarders were removed and the yard was worked from the north end. In September 1985, the yard was halved in size, with sidings Nos. 1–21 being removed, though some were later restored as other parts of the yard were taken out of use. In October 1987, the yard was closed for traffic purposes.

The first Yard Manager was Cliff Tingay, and he remained there for many years, becoming Area Manager from the mid-1960s. He was the longest standing area manager in the Cardiff Division, though probably had retired before the yard was closed.

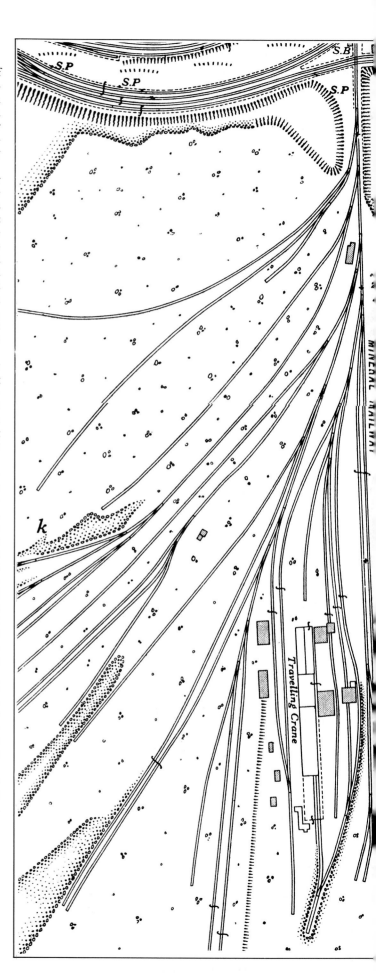

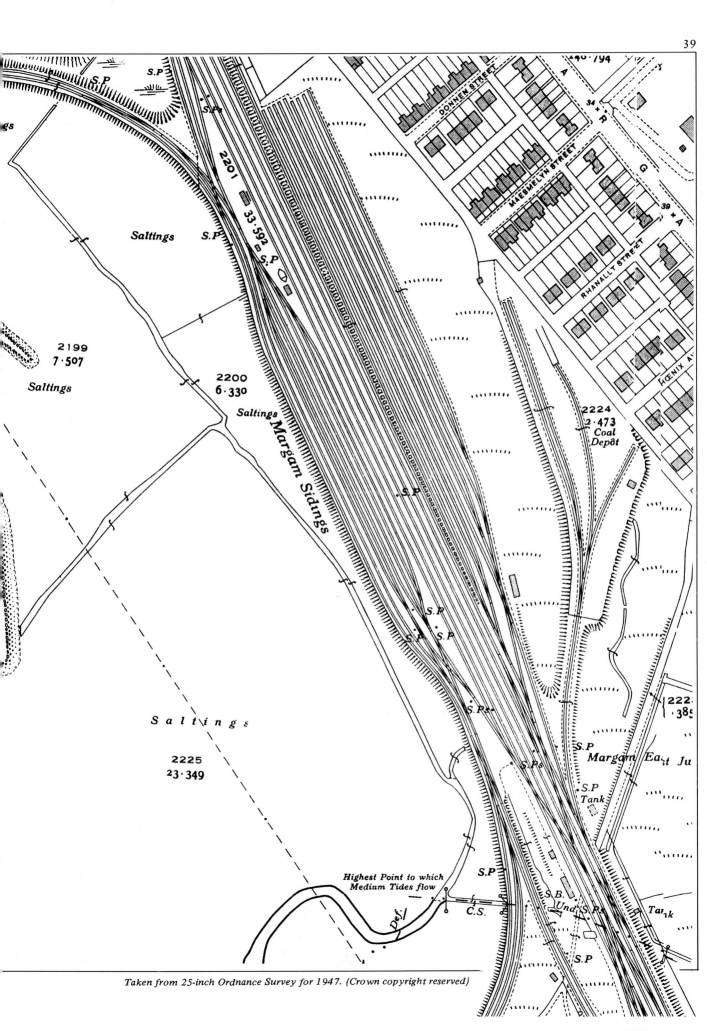

Saltings

S.P

S.P

S.P

2201

33·592

S.P

S.P

Saltings

2199
7·507

Saltings

2200
6·330

Saltings

Margam Sidings

S.P

S.P

S.P
S.P

S.Ps

Saltings

2225
23·349

S.Ps

S.Ps

DONNEN STREET

MAESMELYN STREET

RHANALLT STREET

FŒNIX AV

148·794

34

R

G

39

A

2224
2·473
Coal
Depôt

222
·385

S.P Margam East Ju

S.P
Tank

S.P
Tank

Highest Point to which
Medium Tides flow

Def

C.S.

S.P

S.B.
Und S.Ps

Tank

S.P

A BR (WR) official picture of Margam Hump Marshalling Yard taken during the course of building in July 1959, some eight months before the opening. The picture was taken from the northern throat of the reception sidings at its south end, looking north (i.e. towards Port Talbot). The hump features in the foreground, on the short length of single track to the left of centre, beyond which a single wagon is seen; this fed the 51 sorting sidings. On the extreme left we can see the down through line used by block coal trains running direct from collieries and yards in the Newport and Cardiff Valleys direct to Steel Company of Wales, which were not required to pass through the reception, whilst the up through line curving into the picture from the right was used for return empties. The control tower on the left afforded a complete view across the hump sorting sidings. The main line features on the extreme right-hand edge of the picture, curving to the right as it passed behind the yard water tower. A goods train may just be seen on the Ogmore Vale Extension line in the background, to the right of the water tower, cutting across the complex on its way to Tondu, and the Secondary Sorting Sidings can be seen beyond, to the right of centre. Margam Halt was situated on the main line in the distance, beyond the conical water tower in the yard.

NATIONAL RAILWAY MUSEUM

A sequence of photographs taken at the south end of Margam Sidings, illustrating aspects of the hump yard in operation. They show a '42XX' tank drawing a train of loaded coal on the Up Through alongside the hump (Top); a pannier waiting on the line alongside the hump, with the sorting sidings beyond (Middle); and a wagon running down from the hump on its way to the sidings (Bottom).

42

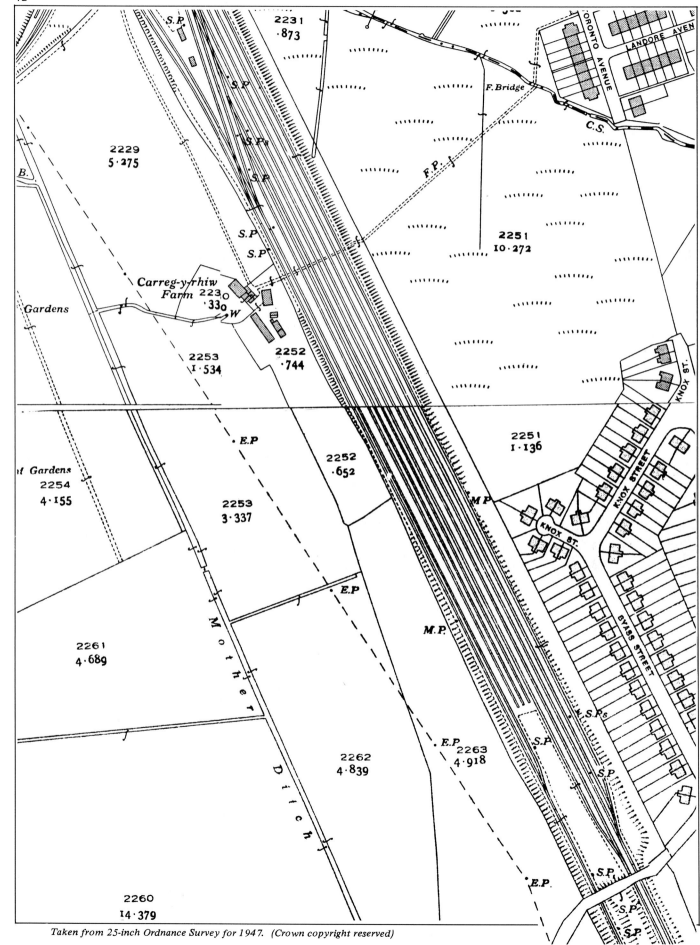

Taken from 25-inch Ordnance Survey for 1947. (Crown copyright reserved)

MARGAM STATION

Located on the main line adjacent to Margam Abbey steelworks, Margam was opened in 1948 for staff, and was served from that time by workmen's trains from Swansea and Porth. The station was unadvertised in public timetables. Construction in the area also involved a new signal box; in 1946, the main-line boxes in the vicinity of Margam had been at Moors, Sidings East (to the south of Margam Sidings) and Sidings West (to the north of Margam Sidings), but with rebuilding in 1950/1, an additional box was placed just to the north of Margam station, and titled East, whilst the Sidings East box was renamed Middle, and Sidings West became the West box. All boxes closed with the opening of Port Talbot Panel Box in September 1963, Margam Halt closing in November 1964.

The scene at Margam East on Saturday, 6th May 1961, looking in the up direction towards Pyle, with track renewal and reballasting in hand; this possibly involved the removal of the nearer trailing connection between the Up and Down Mains, the formation having been superseded by that adjacent to the footbridge beyond. Diesel shunter D3437 was in charge of the leading ballast section of the train, waiting on the Down Main in front of Margam East box, whilst the remainder of the train was parked beyond the footbridge at Margam Halt platform. Llanelly 'Grange' No. 6818 *Hardwick Grange* is seen passing by on the connecting loop between the Down Ogmore Vale Extension line and the Down Main, a manoeuvre probably made necessary by the work on the Down Main. Its train comprised a single passenger brake van; this may well have been a class 'C' milk service for which no milk tanks were available, an arrangement that sometimes happened in order to keep the brake van in its circuit. Margam Halt platform, which can be seen just beyond the footbridge, was opened in 1948 and closed towards the end of 1964.

MICHAEL HALE

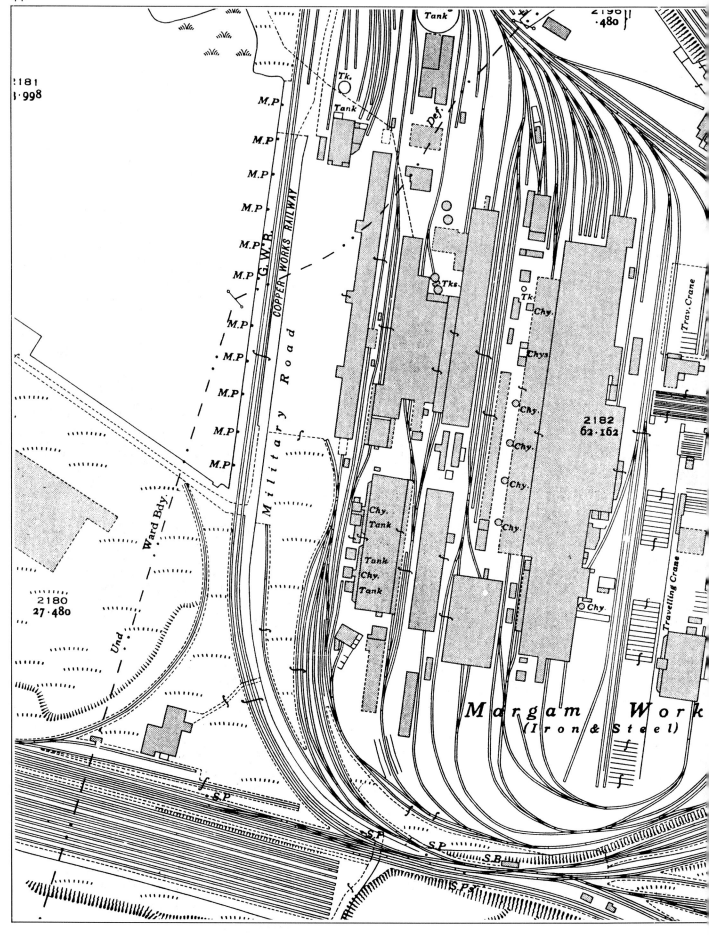

2181
3·998

Tank

Tk.

Tank

M.P

M.P

M.P

M.P

M.P

M.P

M.P

M.P

M.P

M.P

M.P

M.P

G.W.R.

COPPER WORKS RAILWAY

Military Road

Tank

Tks.

Tk.

Chy.

Chys.

Chy.

Chy.

Chy.

Chy.

Chy.

Chy.

Tank

Chy.
Tank

Tank
Chy.
Tank

2182
62·162

Trav. Crane

Travelling Crane

Ward Bdy.

Und.

2180
27·480

S.P.

S.P.

S.P.

S.B.

S.P.

Margam Work
(Iron & Steel)

Def.

2196
·480

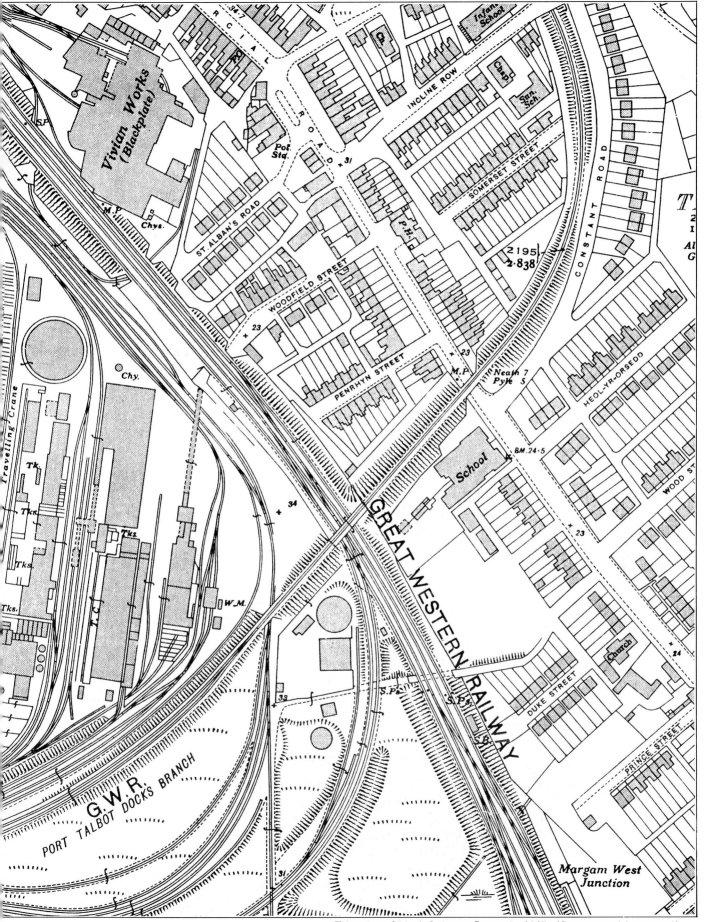

Duffryn Yard shed was located about a half-mile to the east of the main line, alongside the old Port Talbot Railway & Docks line from Pontyrhyll. In the last decade of the GWR, it housed about sixty engines of largely 2–8–0T, 0–6–2T and 0–6–0T designs – mostly of the latter – for goods, shunting and banking purposes, although it did retain a couple of passenger turns. By the late 1950s, '72XX' 2–8–2Ts were also allocated to the shed. The shed's heavy tank engines found themselves on a number of main-line trains, often working as far east as Severn Tunnel Jct. In this view, Nos.3762, 8453 and an unidentified '42XX' are seen on the shed roads in 1959.

F.K. DAVIES, CTY. GW TRUST

DUFFRYN YARD
MPD

A view of the 6–road shed on 14th July 1959, looking west, with, on the right, a '42XX' en route to the turntable at the rear of the shed. The layout was altered in 1931 when the turntable was moved to a site behind the shed, instead of at the right of the shed (as viewed).   H. C. CASSERLEY

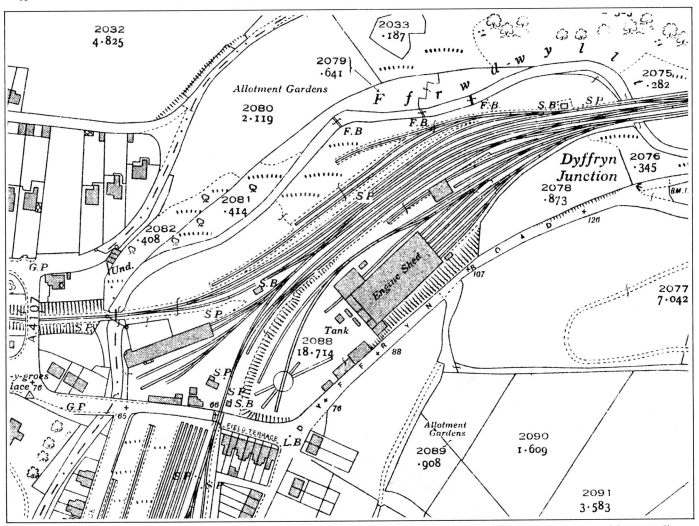

Taken from 25-inch Ordnance Survey for 1947. (Crown copyright reserved)

In this picture, Nos. 5264 and 6616 are seen at their home shed, Duffryn Yard, on 26th September 1958, both undergoing servicing. The line in the background ran to Maesteg and Pontyrhyll (to the right), and to the old Central station and the R & SB line, or Copper Works Jct. and Margam (to the left).

F. K. DAVIES, CTY. GW TRUST

A portrait of No. 6616 outside her home shed on 14th July 1959; she would soon be transferred west to Carmarthen. The raised coal stage road for loco coal vehicles is well illustrated here, with wagons on the holding sidings beyond.

H. C. CASSERLEY

Opened in 1896, Duffryn Yard was both a main line and local shed, located away from the main line at Duffryn Junction, on the former Port Talbot Railway line to Pontyrhyll in the Garw Valley. Duffryn Junction was the point where the Port Talbot Docks Branch (which crossed the main line on an overbridge near Margam West signal box) met the lines from Aberavon Town and Port Talbot Central. Although not relevant here, the Port Talbot Docks branch had two rather evocative places on it just to the south of Duffryn Yard shed, called the 'Chapel of Ease Crossing' and 'Doctors Crossing'.

Access to the shed was provided off the through line to Garth, Lletty Brongu and Pontyrhyll, which abounded in collieries, with entry to the shed being from No. 2 signal box.

A map for 1897 shows a five-road shed with a turntable to the north of the shed, an ash siding and coaling point. In 1900, a carriage shed and sidings were added close to the shed, within the 'V' between the Port Talbot Central and Docks branches.

By 1914, the ash siding had been extended westwards from the turntable, giving a trailing access to a new repair shop attached to the north-western corner of the shed. By 1947, the turntable itself

Servicing taking place at Duffryn Yard on 14th July 1959, with the shed's '72XX' 2–8–2T No. 7244 taking water, her driver turning off the water valve as the engine's side tank gushed over. To the right, a '42XX' was being coaled at the stage.
H. C. CASSERLEY

Taken from just inside the shed entrance on 14th July 1959, this view shows Duffryn '84XX' 0–6–0PT No. 8407, whose crew appear to have been discussing some aspect of the working. No. 6616 is seen on the right, with the coaling plant to the left.
H. C. CASSERLEY

A familiar sight outside the coal stage at Duffryn Yard, with a 2–8–0T and 0–6–0PT in steam on 15th September 1959. The 0–6–0PT, No. 9617, was a Duffryn Yard engine, whilst the 2–8–0 could have been No. 5230, which was recorded as being transferred from store to Duffryn Yard in that autumn.

F. K. DAVIES,
CTY. GW TRUST

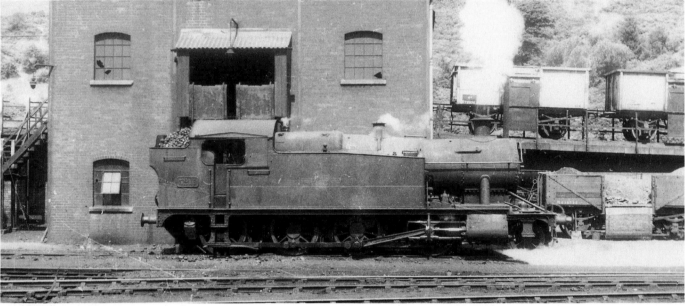

Having been coaled, Ebbw Junction 2–8–0T No. 5216, with drain cocks open, was steaming to the rear of the shed to turn, prior to working back to Newport, on 14th July 1959. Empty loco coal wagons can be seen with their side doors still open after sweeping out, and these would be dropped down by gravity feed to be disposed of at the east end of the depot. The narrowness of the bunkers of tank engines required a fairly accurate positioning in order to get most of the coal from the tubs into them.

H. C. CASSERLEY

had been moved to the west of the shed, with five spurs off, though the 'trailing' connection to the repair shop had been removed.

Access to the main line from Duffryn Yard shed was via Duffryn Junction and Aberavon Town, from where the line curved round to join the main line just west of Port Talbot General. Alternatively, engines could run via the Port Talbot Docks branch to Copper Works Jct., and thence to Port Talbot or Margam.

About 60 engines were normally allocated to Duffryn Yard, which, during the 1950s, were all tank engines, made up mainly of '42XX', '56XX', '57XX' and '84XX' types, though a few '28XX' and '72XX' were also there sometimes. At the end of 1953, Duffryn Yard's allocation stood at 62 engines:

2	'28XX' 2-8-0s
1	'72XX' 2-8-2T
8	'42XX' 2-8-0Ts
7	'56XX' 0-6-2Ts
2	ex-Rhymney 0-6-2Ts
29	'57XX' 0-6-0PTs, including 9 steam braked-only '67XXs' for dock shunting
16	'94XX' 0-6-0PTs

The two ex-RR engines were allocated in June 1934 as replacements for the many ex-Port Talbot and Rhondda & Swansea Bay engines withdrawn during that decade, with '57XXs' replacing the remainder. The last Port Talbot engines at Duffryn Yard were 0-6-2Ts Nos. 184, condemned in October 1948, and 188, withdrawn in September 1947. The last of the indigenous R & SB types were withdrawn from Duffryn and Danygraig in 1936.

In 1959, there were five daily duties for '56XXs', one for a '72XX' and nine for the '42XXs', as well as many shunting and local tripping turns. The shed's '42s', together with the '72s' and '28s' when allocated, worked regularly on the main line as far east as Severn Tunnel Junction.

After the opening of Margam Yard, many services originated there; in 1962, there were around two dozen main-line departures daily from the yard, all steam-worked eastward. However, these soon came to be worked by diesel power (classes '37' and '47'), whilst diesel shunters took over the yard duties, leading to the swift decline in demand for engines from Duffryn Yard. The shed closed in March 1964, and the carriage sidings in the same year with the withdrawal of passenger services between Treherbert and Swansea.

This view of the coal stage road at Duffryn Yard shed shows one of the Carmarthen RODs No. 3010, which had presumably worked in on a freight from West Wales and was sharing company with a '28XX' and '42XX' on shed. No. 3010 was withdrawn in March 1956.

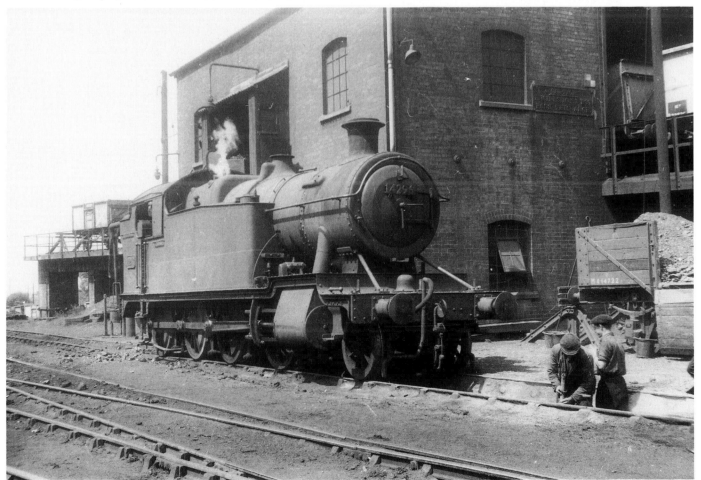

Duffryn 2–8–0T No. 4296 being coaled on 14th July 1959 as two shed labourers carried on with the unenviable task of clearing out the ash and clinker from the pit, and depositing it in the open wagon behind. The extent of the holding area for loaded engine coal wagons can be appreciated in this view, with room for five or six vehicles clear of the stage.

H. C. CASSERLEY

In this view of Duffryn Yard shed, taken in September 1962, Nos. 9456 and 3682 (both Duffryn Yard, 87B) are seen in the foreground, with No. 6680 (Landore) at the coaling stage. The '57XX' tank was a long-time Swindon engine, and had recently been transferred to Duffryn Yard.

F. K. DAVIES, CTY. GW TRUST

No. 5249 being filled with water at Duffryn Yard shed on 1st November 1956. The '42s' were mainly utilised on trips from Margam to Tondu, Cardiff, Rogerstone, East Usk and Severn Tunnel Jct., and sometimes on trains destined for England, though usually only as far as Cardiff.
F. K. DAVIES, CTY. GW TRUST

Another view of No. 7244 which, having been coaled and watered, was now reversing off the shed spur past the tiny Duffryn Junction No. 2 box. As the track between the shed and Port Talbot swung round in a half circle, she would be bound for a down line service on the main line if routed via Aberavon Town and General stations, or if via Chapel of Ease and the PT Docks branch, she could work head-up towards Cardiff when she entered the Margam complex. The start of the gradient to the coal stage road can be seen to the left of the engine's bunker. H. C. CASSERLEY

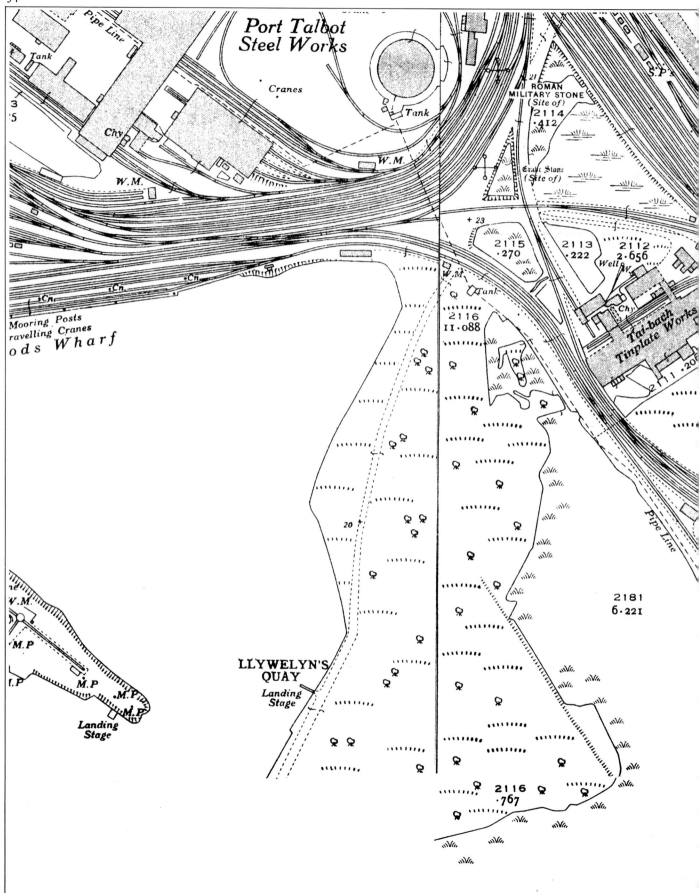

Port Talbot
Steel Works

Pipe Line

Tank

Cranes

Chy

Tank

W.M.

W.M.

Cn

Mooring Posts
ravelling Cranes
ods Wharf

ROMAN
MILITARY STONE
(Site of)
2114
.412

Crane Stone
(Site of)

+ 23

2115
.270

2113
.222

2112
2.656

Well

W.M.

Tank

2116
11.088

Tai-bach
Tinplate Works

20

2181
6.221

Pipe Line

W.M.

M.P

M.P

M.P

M.P

M.P

Landing
Stage

LLYWELYN'S
QUAY
Landing
Stage

2116
.767

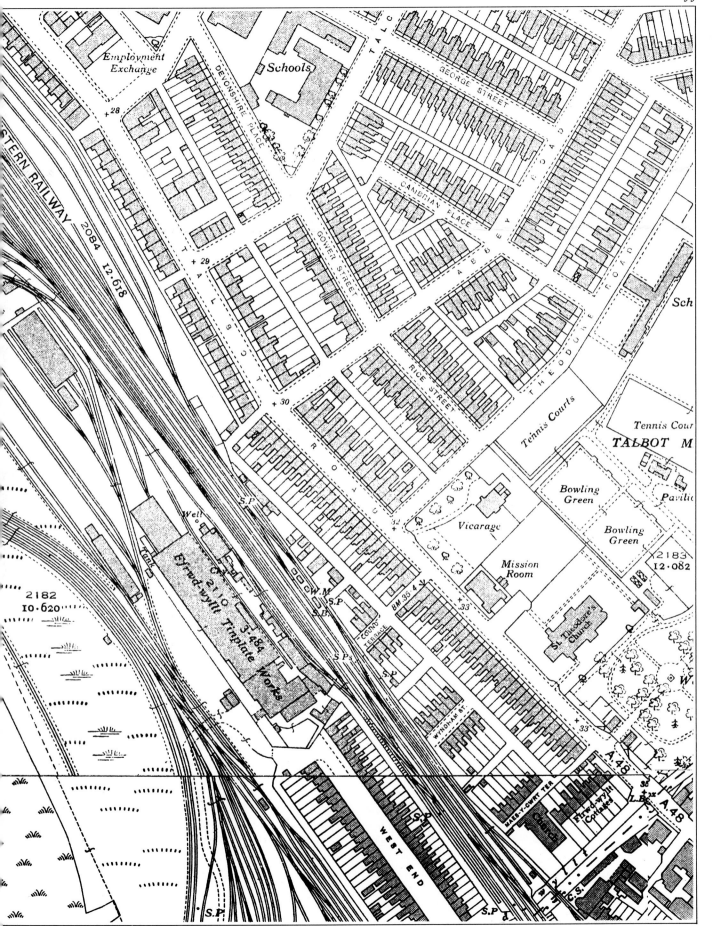

Taken from 25-inch Ordnance Survey. (Crown copyright reserved)

The main line through Port Talbot ran in an approximately south-east/north-west direction, although this was represented in railway protocol as east-west. This view, looking in the up direction, was taken from the footbridge at the Margam (south-east) end of the platforms at Port Talbot General on 24th July 1959, with the goods shed on the left and Port Talbot Middle Signal Box on the right. The box was renewed in about April 1960 but was closed in September 1963 when the new Panel Box was opened on the same site. On the Down Goods line, a light 42XX was awaiting the road with a '43XX' on a short goods service beyond. Both would need to run through the station on the Down Main, highlighting the bottle-neck conditions which prevailed until the rebuilding in 1963, when a Down Relief line ran through to the west of the Down Main. However, this easement only applied as far as Port Talbot West (just beyond the end of the platform), where the bridge over the River Avon precluded further track expansion. The wagons behind the water tower would probably all have been traffic to or from the Steelworks, parts of which can just be seen in the gloom beyond.   NATIONAL RAILWAY MUSEUM

PORT TALBOT

Port Talbot station opened along with the South Wales line on 18th June 1850, and was located in the western part of the town, close to the small estuary of the River Avon (Afan). Although the tidal harbour here had been used for trade over many centuries, the first of the dock facilities was not opened until 1837.

Approaching Margam from the east, the main line leaves its mainly westerly alignment and swings around to run in a north-westerly direction to follow the coast of Swansea Bay as it approaches Port Talbot. The Great Western adopted 'East' and 'West' suffixes for their signal boxes and in general working references in consideration of the direction of the route as a whole, regardless of any true geographical bearing at any individual locations. Thus, from Port Talbot, facing Margam was in the south-easterly direction, and Briton Ferry the north-west.

A map of the Port Talbot station area of the 1870s shows the main line crossed by the Oakwood Mineral Railway at the point where the level crossing at the south end of the station would later be, and by the Cwmavon Mineral Railway where the R & SB line would be developed to the north of the station, alongside the river; both crossings were effected by flat junctions. The Oakwood line continued into Port Talbot Dock, where it was crossed by the Great Western Port Talbot Dock branch, which fed out of a group of sidings to the south of the station, alongside the entrance to Taibach Tinplate Works, and across the line from the Vivian's Works Siding. The goods shed was in the same position as in future years, immediately to the south of the station, on the up side. The Mansel Tinplate Works was located north of the station with connections with both the GWR and the Cwmavon lines. The station platforms were lengthened, widened and raised in 1879.

The Great Western station was renamed Port Talbot & Aberavon in June 1897, whilst the signal boxes became East, Middle and West at around the same time, instead of Nos. 1, 2 and 3. This was all tied in with the opening of the Port Talbot Railway's Port Talbot Central station in February 1898, the site being just to the north-east of the GWR station, and connected with the Oakwood Mineral line. The two stations were separated by the main road.

Earlier, in November 1885, the R & SB line's Aberavon station had opened with the completion of its line between Cymmer and Aberavon, which was continued across the Great Western line and on to Briton Ferry in December 1893; this station again went through a number of name changes, from Aberavon to Aberavon & Port Talbot in 1891, to Port Talbot (Aberavon) in 1895, and finally to Aberavon Town in 1924, at which time the GWR station became Port Talbot General.

By 1899, the sidings between the R & SB line and the GW line had increased in number and spread to the area behind (to the east of) the Great Western station, whilst the down sidings on the southern approaches to the station were also extended in 1913–14.

Port Talbot in the first months of nationalisation, with Bath Road 'Castle' No. 5067 *St. Fagans Castle* waiting at the up platform on Saturday, 27th March 1948. Bath Road's 'Castles' worked into Wales as far as Cardiff for the most part, though they ran to Swansea on one turn: a long-standing roster through the 1940s specified the Bristol engine for the 7.52 a.m. Cardiff (5.50 a.m. ex-Bristol, later 7.20 a.m. Newport) to Swansea, though by the early 1950s it was used on the 7.35 a.m. Cardiff to Swansea semi-fast (for Neyland,). The 'Castle' returned to Cardiff with the 10.15 a.m. Carmarthen to Gloucester train (11.33 a.m. Swansea) in the mid-1940s, and by the early 1950s, the 8.20 a.m. Neyland to Paddington train (10.50 a.m. Swansea). Port Talbot station was located alongside the dock and industrial area – which was to its south-west – with the town on the eastern side of the tracks. To the right can be seen Port Talbot goods shed, on the far side of the level crossing.

F. K. DAVIES, CTY GW TRUST

In the years leading up to the Great War, the station area had come to be dominated by the Port Talbot Steelworks, which had developed in the area directly to the west of the station with a large complex of plant and sidings, extending down to the North Bank of the Old Dock. Ten new sidings immediately to the south of the station, for the steelworks, had also been laid in by 1917. With the later development of Margam Steelworks, the Port Talbot Steelworks closed and the site was cleared, though some concerns maintained rail-connected sites until 1970.

The crossing of the R & SB route on the level at Port Talbot was the cause of increasing interference in the working of main-line traffic, and during the early 1920s a scheme was proposed to deal with the problem. This involved the construction of an overbridge to carry the R & SB line over the Great Western; moving the GWR station northwards to that point; and building a new R & SB station immediately to the east of the new bridge on an extended double-track section, with a passenger connection to the new GWR station by a stairway. Port Talbot Railway trains would run

Port Talbot General station seen in the early 1950s, looking up towards Margam and Bridgend, showing the substantial canopies attached to the three main structures. A diesel railcar can just be seen in the up sidings beyond platform No. 1, with a large body of what were probably PW men standing on the adjacent main-line trackwork beyond the crossing. This may have been a Sunday.
L & GRP

Landore 'Castle' No. 4095 *Harlech Castle* running into Port Talbot General with the eight-coach up 'South Wales Pullman' on Tuesday, 15th May 1956. This was the longest resident 'Castle' at Landore shed, allocated there in August 1936, and remaining until the mileage equalisation exercise in 1957, when she moved to Penzance. *Harlech Castle* also enjoyed the almost unique distinction of never being allocated to Old Oak Common, having been a West Country engine from new (in 1926) until 1936, and returning there from 1957 to 1962, although she did spend her final days in the London Division, at Reading, in 1962.

E. R. MOUNTFORD/R. C. RILEY COLLECTION

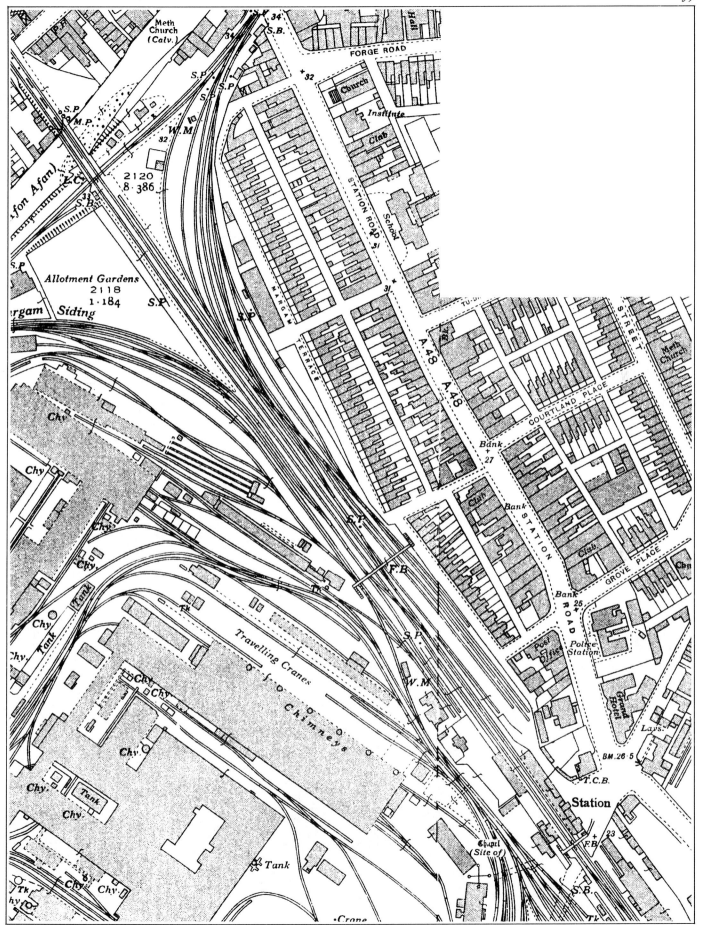

Taken from 25-inch Ordnance Survey. (Crown copyright reserved)

Landore 0–6–2T No. 6650 heading a down mixed freight from nearby Margam Yard along the Down Main past Port Talbot goods shed on Thursday, 9th March 1961. The train, formed of mineral and tank wagons, carried the class '9', (old 'K') lamps – probably the 1.30 p.m. pilot trip to Swansea East Dock. The new arrangement of the Up and Down Mains and Reliefs – including the gap between the Up and Down pairs on the approach to the new island platform, seen here – was sandwiched between the new Panel Box (the site of which is on the extreme right of the picture) and the goods shed. Most of the sidings off to the right would all be recovered between 1965–9.

into the R & SB station, and that company's Central station would close for passengers. In addition, a new double-track loop would run from a junction to the south of the Great Western station to another on the R & SB, to the west of the new bridge, allowing direct running over that part of the R & SB to and from Briton Ferry. This ambitious scheme was not proceeded with.

A new – but temporary – box to replace the old Port Talbot Middle was provided in 1960, and in 1961 work began on a new station in the form of an island platform. The original up platform was demolished, and a new, temporary up platform constructed using the existing sidings on the east side of the former station, and

converting these to running lines; this effectively created three up loop lines, one of which served the new platform. The former down platform remained in use for down trains, though for the first few months this was very restricted due to the demolition going on. The new island platform came into use on 22nd September 1963, on which date the new Panel Box was also commissioned, and all the former R & SB lines and connections were all taken out of use. Up and Down Relief lines now ran outside the respective main lines, but ended at the bridge over the River Avon, the location of the former Port Talbot West box.

A panoramic view from the footbridge at the south (up) end of the station, looking north, and showing Old Oak Common's double-chimney 'Castle' No.7010 *Avondale Castle* standing at Port Talbot's temporary up platform with the 11.10 a.m. Milford Haven to Paddington (Train A90 – 1.30 p.m. Swansea, 3.0 p.m. Cardiff) on 9th March 1961. This train was due out of Port Talbot at 2.0 p.m., calling at Bridgend, Cardiff and Newport en route to London, conveying through coaches from Pembroke Dock as well as Milford, with the usual dining cars from Swansea. The temporary station arrangement had the old down and up mains (still serving as such) and an additional short up loop; the old (and now, temporary) Up Main would survive as the Up Relief.

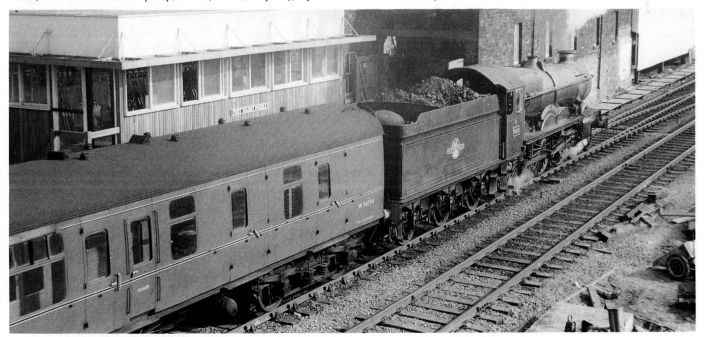

Avondale Castle departing over the level crossing with the 11.10 a.m. Milford on 9th March, past the temporary signal box next to the goods shed, which replaced the Middle box on the opposite side of the running lines. Entering traffic in July 1948 at Oxford for a Paddington, Wolverhampton and Worcester duty, No. 7010 was initially given an experimental light green livery. The engine was transferred to Old Oak in October 1952, and survived in traffic until March 1964.

Two views of Shrewsbury Standard Class '5' No. 73091 working an up class 8 ('H') freight through the temporary up platform road on 9th March 1961. This train may have been the 8.25 a.m. Swansea (East Depot) to Crewe (Gresty Lane), which was worked by a Salop loco in the early 1960s, as were the 2.20 a.m. and 8.40 p.m. trains from East Depot to Coton Hill or Stafford (usually '48XXXs'). There were still a significant number of wooden mineral wagons in traffic at this time, and one may be seen within the formation. These views show the northern and southern aspects during the rebuilding. A new connection had been installed in the up main at the far west end to allow trains to gain access to the temporary platform line. The goods shed and level crossing still remained at the east end of the site.

Another scene at Port Talbot during the re-building of the station as part of the introduction of Multiple Aspect Signalling in 1963, and the creation of an island platform to handle all up and down passenger trains. The east face of the new island platform was used for down traffic during the rebuilding, and here we see the 8.55 a.m. Paddington to Pembroke Dock and Neyland service waiting behind Landore double-chimney 'Castle' No. 5016 *Montgomery Castle* on Thursday, 9th March 1961.

During the building of the new island platform, up trains were handled at a temporary platform alongside the road, which can be seen to the left of the running lines. A view from the station footbridge shows the down 'Pembroke Coast Express', the 10.55 a.m. Paddington to Pembroke Dock, running through the down platform on 9th March 1961; this train was non-stop between Cardiff and Swansea, and was allowed 68 minutes for the 46 miles. The engine, Landore's 'Castle' No. 5062 *Earl of Shaftesbury*, was in the usual pristine Landore condition for a top link engine.

Coming off the Rhondda & Swansea Bay lines at the north end of the station, Duffryn Yard Pannier No. 9799, carrying a target number 'H14', was bringing a short train of mineral wagons towards the main line on 9th March 1961. Mynydd Dinas, with its peak at 845ft above sea level, dominates the scene.

The completed island platform can be partially seen in this picture of a woebegone 2–8–0T No. 5239 heading a train of bogie bolsters along the new Up Relief line through the station on 23rd March 1963. The engine was withdrawn from traffic during the following month, though it still languished in storage outside the old works at Barry some 18 months later.
F. K. DAVIES, CTY GW TRUST

The view looking in the down direction from the station footbridge, showing the 12.5 p.m. Milford Haven to Paddington (Train A11, 2.30 p.m. ex-Swansea, 4p.m. ex-Cardiff) on the new crossover into the temporary up platform on 9th March 1961. The engine, Old Oak Common's Castle No. 5087 *Tintern Abbey*, was working back to Paddington with a train of mostly maroon Mark 1 stock; in the winter schedules, this engine had worked out overnight with the 8.55 p.m. Paddington to Neyland as far as Swansea. The former Rhondda & Swansea Bay lines may be seen behind the leading coaches of the train, curving around to the right from East Jct. to meet the old company's Swansea to Cymmer and Treherbert route at Plough Jct, Aberavon Town station.

The layout at Port Talbot West was included in the September 1963 modifications and, in preparation for implementation, the trackwork linking the main line with the former R & SB line to Aberavon Town was cut back to just two running lines with two stop-blocked sidings on either side, as can be seen in this view taken on 6th January 1961. The former R & SB line below Plough Junction, just south of Aberavon Town station and signal box, was closed in December 1962, thus enabling the flat junction with the SWML to be removed. The main line was just behind the cameraman at this point.   NATIONAL RAILWAY MUSEUM

The view looking towards West box from the (temporary) down platform on Friday, 1st September 1961, with Canton 'Britannia' No. 70027 *Rising Star* on the 11.55 a.m. Paddington to Milford and Pembroke service during the final months of 'Britannia' presence at Canton. The tracks on the left would become the new Down Main and Down Relief lines; to their left we see the truncated remains of lines serving the former Port Talbot Steelworks, and Margam and Mansel Tin Plate Works. As part of the introduction of MAS, the layout was completely altered to provide a freight loop on each side of the island, outside the platform roads, though at the west end these terminated just beyond the station, as can be seen in this view.

In 1954, the bridge over the River Avon at Port Talbot West was renewed, and this 10th March 1954 view looking south (up) from the north side of the level crossing shows the new bridge in position. Also just visible between the gates is the R & SB line, which crossed the SWML at right-angles on the flat, with West box beyond. The Port Talbot steelworks are prominent in the background. The wagons standing beyond the crossing gates on the up side were on the track which became the Up Relief line in the modifications of 1963, while the new Down Relief line rejoined the main near the Down Home signal in the centre of the picture.

NATIONAL RAILWAY MUSEUM

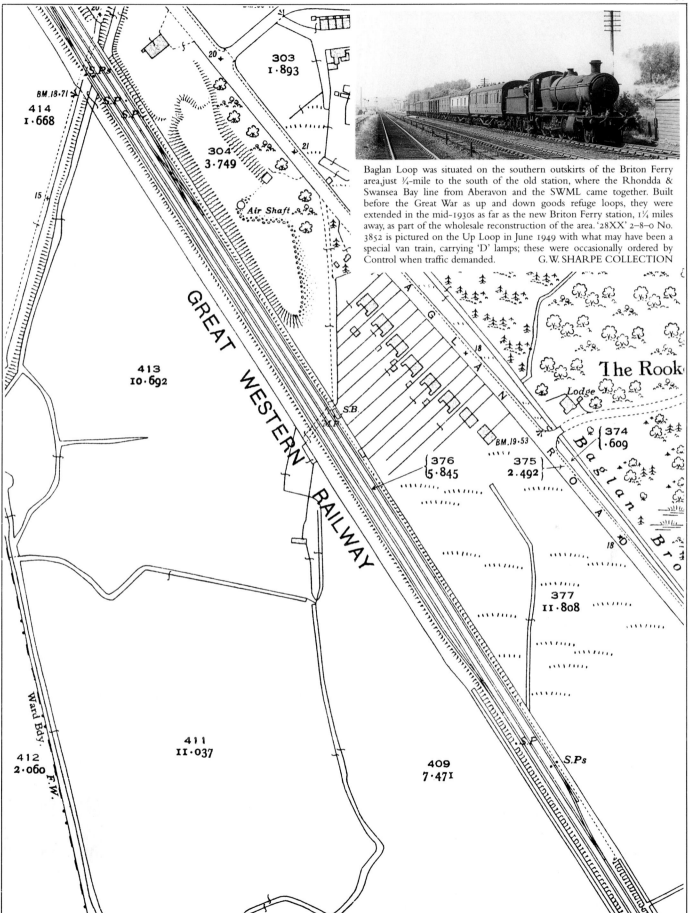

Baglan Loop was situated on the southern outskirts of the Briton Ferry area, just ¾-mile to the south of the old station, where the Rhondda & Swansea Bay line from Aberavon and the SWML came together. Built before the Great War as up and down goods refuge loops, they were extended in the mid-1930s as far as the new Briton Ferry station, 1¼ miles away, as part of the wholesale reconstruction of the area. '28XX' 2–8–0 No. 3852 is pictured on the Up Loop in June 1949 with what may have been a special van train, carrying 'D' lamps; these were occasionally ordered by Control when traffic demanded.　　　　G. W. SHARPE COLLECTION

Taken from 25-inch Ordnance Survey for 1935. (Crown copyright reserved)

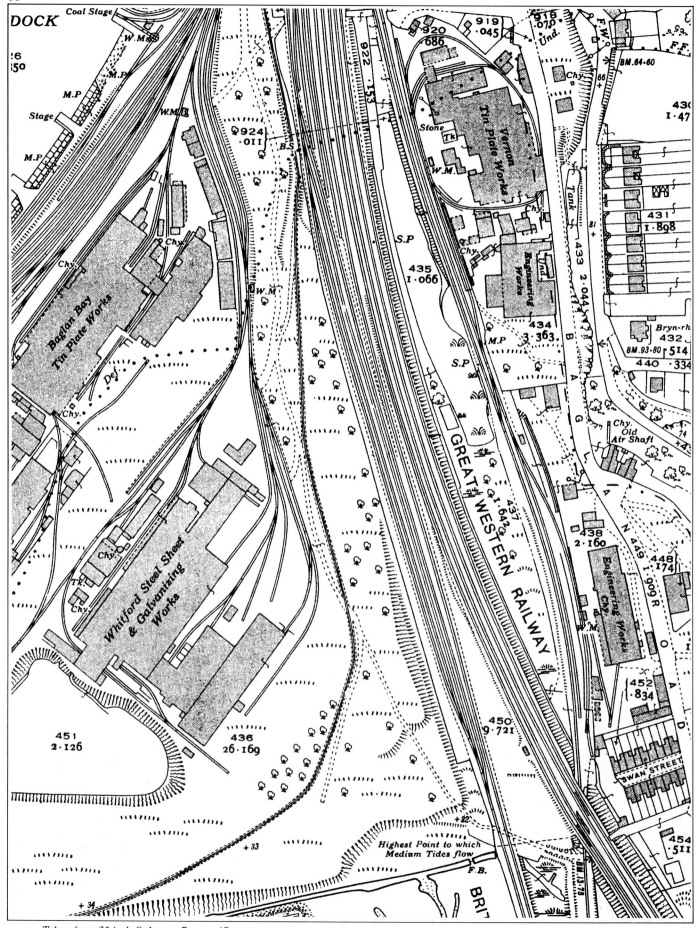

68

Taken from 25-inch Ordnance Survey. (Crown copyright reserved)

BRITON FERRY

Briton Ferry is just under 3 miles to the north of Port Talbot. On its approach to Briton Ferry, the railway swings from its former north-westerly alignment to a northerly one as it follows the eastern side of the River Neath's valley. The original South Wales Railway station was opened in September 1850 on the southern outskirts of the town, adjacent to the north end of the dock, and comprised up and down platforms. Early goods traffic centred around Briton Ferry dock, opened in 1861, with coal shipment berths on the quays. Originally, there was a network of tramways serving the dock, bringing coal from local pits, which included the Wern Pistyll and Swan Collieries. The layout on the GWR which ran along the north corner of the Dock was simply up and down main lines in 1870, but three stop-blocked sidings had been added on the down side by 1898.

The site of Vernon Jct., Briton Ferry, on 26th August 1959, showing the up Rhondda & Swansea Bay line to Aberavon on the left, the four up and down mains and reliefs in the centre, and the down R & SB from Aberavon immediately to their right. Originally, the R & SB ran as a double line (up and down) on the left, but this was changed to that shown in the 1935 rebuilding. The sidings on the right, where Neath pannier tank No. 7737 is seen shunting wagons on the furthest line, were originally exchange sidings between the two companies. From the 1935 rebuilding, the up and down R & SB lines were separated; the up line to Aberavon Town can be seen diverging to the left, whilst the down line ran in under the right-hand side of the signal gantry, the two lines diverging at Baglan Jct., some ¾-mile to the south. MICHAEL HALE

The view looking south towards Port Talbot, showing the Up ex-Rhondda & Swansea Bay single line on the left, descending to cross beneath the main lines, then the four running lines, with the Down R & SB to their right. The R & SB line from Aberavon followed a path closer to the coast than the GWR main line. Here Canton 'Britannia' No. 70022 *Tornado* was heading the 10.35 a.m. Kensington to Whitland milk empties along the Down Main, running with only four empty tanks and a brake, on 1st September 1961. The sidings on the right took traffic for the Albion Steelworks, and previously the other industrial concerns around Briton Ferry Dock, and now lead into BP Chemicals, Baglan Bay.

70

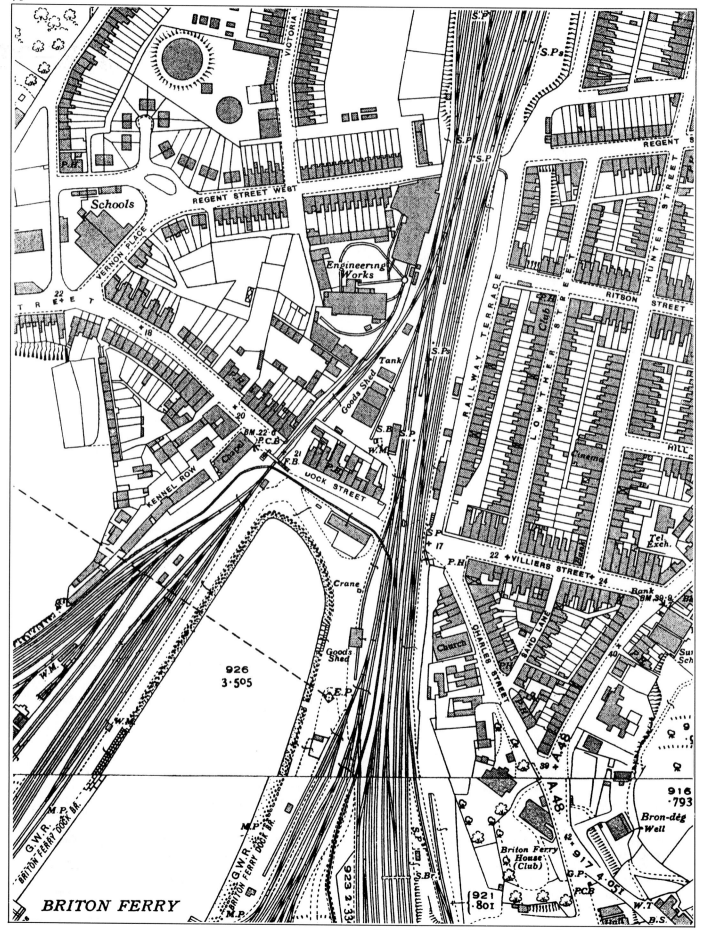

BRITON FERRY

Taken from 25-inch Ordnance Survey. (Crown copyright reserved)

On the southern approaches to Briton Ferry, the main line gradually turned to run northwards. This view, looking in the Down direction (north) on 26th August 1959, shows Landore's 2–6–2T No. 4106 accelerating away along the Up Main with a five-coach Swansea to Porthcawl service, while Swansea East Dock 0–6–0PT No. 8414 was coasting along the Up Relief line with a wagon of sleepers. No. 7737 can also be seen outside Briton Ferry signal box.　　　MICHAEL HALE

This photograph, taken from outside Briton Ferry box, shows Neath '42XX' 2–8–0T No. 5209 heading towards Port Talbot along the Up Main with a class S ('D') train of fitted tinplate vans from Trostre or Velindre tinplate works, on 23rd March 1963. The platform elevation of the old Briton Ferry station building at the first site (closed in 1935) features in the background.　　　F. K. DAVIES, CTY GW TRUST

As at other locations in South Wales, heavy industries were soon established around the dock area. The Briton Ferry Ironworks was located on the west side of the dock, and was in operation by the 1870s, whilst the Baglan Bay Tinplate Works opened on land on the east side of the dock in 1890, and the Albion Steel Works alongside in 1892. By 1898, industrial growth had continued on the west side of the dock, and in addition to Briton Ferry Steelworks (the former ironworks), there was now also the Villiers Tinplate Works, the Gwalia Tinplate Works and the Cambrian Coke Works. These were joined by the Baldwins Sintering Works during the Great War. To the east of the dock, the Whitford Steelworks (Whitford Steel Sheet & Galvanising Co.) had opened in 1911. Briton Ferry Dock was also used extensively by the Vale of Neath Railway before the construction of their direct line into Swansea Docks from Neath.

An 1880s map shows two nests of five sidings to the north of the passenger station on the down side, and also a Welsh Steam Works for patent fuel, and an 'Engine House'; by 1898, the latter had been taken over by the Glyncorrwg Wagon Repair Works, which by 1914 had become the North Central Wagon repairs.

In 1883, the original Briton Ferry East signal box was located a short distance to the south of the down platform of the passenger station, but was replaced in that year by a new box on the south end of the platform. In 1892. this was in turn replaced by another box immediately to the north of the down platform.

At the same time, Briton Ferry West box was located in the area of the sidings, to the east of the running lines.

During 1893, the Great Western was joined in Briton Ferry by the extension of the Rhondda & Swansea Bay Railway from Port Talbot/Aberavon, and a small station was built alongside (and to the

Landore 'Castle' No. 7028 *Cadbury Castle* passing Briton Ferry box, a half-mile to the south of the 1935 station, with the 2.30 p.m. Neyland to Paddington (5.30 p.m. ex-Swansea, 7.0 p.m. Cardiff) on 1st September 1961, passing through the site of the old 1850s Briton Ferry station. New in June 1950, No. 7028 spent nearly the whole of its working life at Landore, only moving to Llanelly when Landore closed for dieselisation in September 1961. The engine was running with the small reporting number board fixed to the top of the smokebox and not with the normal frame, whilst her train was formed with a maroon set of Mark 1 coaches.

Fish had been a regular traffic along the South Wales main line since the 19th century, particularly from Old Milford (renamed Milford Haven in 1906). Here, an Up train, the 3.50 p.m. Milford Haven to Weymouth fish, was recorded on 1st September 1961 behind Landore 'Castle' No. 4094 *Dynevor Castle*, which worked the train to Canton. Although fish might not seem to rate alongside passengers as requiring priority treatment, it was a perishable commodity, like fruit and milk, and was therefore given a passenger-rated operating category. Passenger engines were therefore utilised on fish trains.

More of the sidings are visible in this photograph taken on the evening of 1st September 1961, which shows ex-works 2–8–2T No. 7221 from Aberdare shed on the Down Main with a train of coke, although the head of the train was formed with a 'Lowmac' and a couple of empty mineral wagons. On the sidings, Swansea East Dock's 0–6–2T No. 5675 was shunting various loaded and empty wagons.

east of) the GWR site. A short distance to the south, the R & SB also opened a short branch off its main line, at Baglan, running to the west of the GWR line to serve the dock. Having run close to the coast on its way north from Aberavon, and after parting company with its branch to the docks at Baglan, the R & SB passed beneath the GWR line, then swung northwards to its station.

In 1894, the R & SB main line was extended again, this time from Briton Ferry to Swansea, running to the east of the Great Western line through the town to Court Sart.

A new goods shed was opened in 1894 to the west of the passenger station.

Both East and West signal boxes were closed in 1915/16, and were replaced by a new Briton Ferry box, again located at the north end of the down passenger platform. This box was itself replaced in the 1930s rebuilding by another which stood well to the west of the main lines, and this can be seen in several of the photographs we have used.

Overtaken by the facilities on offer at Swansea Dock, and by the expanding steelworks at Margam, Briton Ferry Dock closed in 1940. Of the industries surrounding it, Briton Ferry Steel works and the Whitford Steel and Galvanising Co. were taken over by Richard Thomas & Baldwins in 1947, and closed in 1964. Baglan Bay Tinplate Works siding agreement was terminated in 1958, around which time the other tinplate works were probably also closed, ousted by the large and modern works at Trostre and

Velindre. The Albion Steelworks (taken over by Duponts) closed in 1979. The cleared site of the former Briton Ferry steelworks on the west side of the dock was taken over by T.W. Ward for wagon repair and scrapping. On the more positive side, the BP Chemical Works at Baglan Bay, east of the dock complex, opened in 1963 as British Hydrocarbon Chemicals, is still in production.

NEW STATION

In 1934/5, major rebuilding took place at Briton Ferry, with a four-track Main and Relief line arrangement replacing the former double track from Baglan Loop box in the south to the north end of the siding nests. In addition, a new pair of goods avoiding lines ran to the west of these, onwards from the old station site.

The old passenger station was replaced by a new one a quarter-of-a-mile further north, opening in July 1935. This comprised two island platforms, with the Up and Down Main lines passing between them, and the Up and Down Reliefs along their outer faces. An Up Avoiding Line from Swansea R & SB ran though the eastern part of the new station, to the outside of which were the main station buildings alongside the public road, connected to the platforms by a lengthy footbridge.

R & SB trains initially continued to use their original single-platform station to the south, but from mid-September 1935 they also began to use the new station. In order to rationalize their movements within the new trackwork formations, the old R & SB lines

The layout outside Briton Ferry box can be seen again in this picture of the up 'Pembroke Coast Express', 1.5 p.m. Pembroke Dock to Paddington, on Monday, 27th June 1960. The engine, Landore's No. 4094 *Dynevor Castle*, was 3 months out of Swindon after a Heavy Intermediate repair, and so still on top link duties. Leaving Swansea at 3.45 p.m., the 'Castle' worked this train to Paddington (due 7.50 p.m.), calling only at Cardiff and Newport en route. It returned to Swansea the following morning with the 8.50 a.m. Paddington, the 'South Wales Pullman'. Pointwork in the foreground, and that passing under the middle of the train, marked the beginning of the goods running lines, which paralleled the main line to the west through the station area to Court Sart and Neath Jct. (R & SB) signal boxes.

An '84XX' 0-6-0T running along the R & SB Down line with the four-coach 5.40 p.m. Treherbert to Neath train on 1st September 1961, and about to join the Down Relief line. At this time, there were six or seven through passenger trains on the R & SB in each direction between Treherbert and Neath or Swansea, taking around 1½ hours for the 28 miles of the entire route, with DMUs on most.

'42XX' 2-8-0T No. 5242 shunting in the yard to the south of Briton Ferry old station, with the down gantry silhouetted against a clear sky. Briton Ferry dock was a short distance off to the right of the picture at this point. A cross-country DMU set can be seen on the main lines.

F. K. DAVIES, CTY GW TRUST

The 11.55 a.m. Paddington to West Wales train running on the Down Main behind Old Oak Common 'Castle' No. 7010 *Avondale Castle* on 27th June 1960. The turn was shown as Landore's, balancing the overnight 10.5 p.m. Milford Haven to Paddington sleeper, but summer diagrams could change due to the insertion of dated trains.

A grimy '56XX' No. 5673 from Neath shed running along the up main with the 5.5 p.m. Swansea to Porthcawl five-coach train on 1st September 1961. The combination would return with the 6.35 p.m. Porthcawl to Swansea. At this time, there were three daily through trains between Swansea and Porthcawl each way in the summer, with an additional service on Saturdays, and a couple during the winter, all using the western curve at Pyle.

Swindon's double-chimney 'Castle' No. 5064 *Bishop's Castle* on the gentle curve past Briton Ferry box with the 3.50 p.m. Whitland to Kensington milk on 1st September 1961, the load, around 17 tanks and a passenger brake van, totalling around 500 tons. The twin canopies of the 1935 Briton Ferry station can just be seen in the distance, some half-mile away, although the old 'station' signal box remained at its former location, on the left. Beyond the engine, the stone buttress of the old R & SB line bridge can be seen, showing the alignment of that line at this point in relation to the Great Western. The two stations were adjacent, with the R & SB platform on the far side of the single R & SB line from the GWR station.

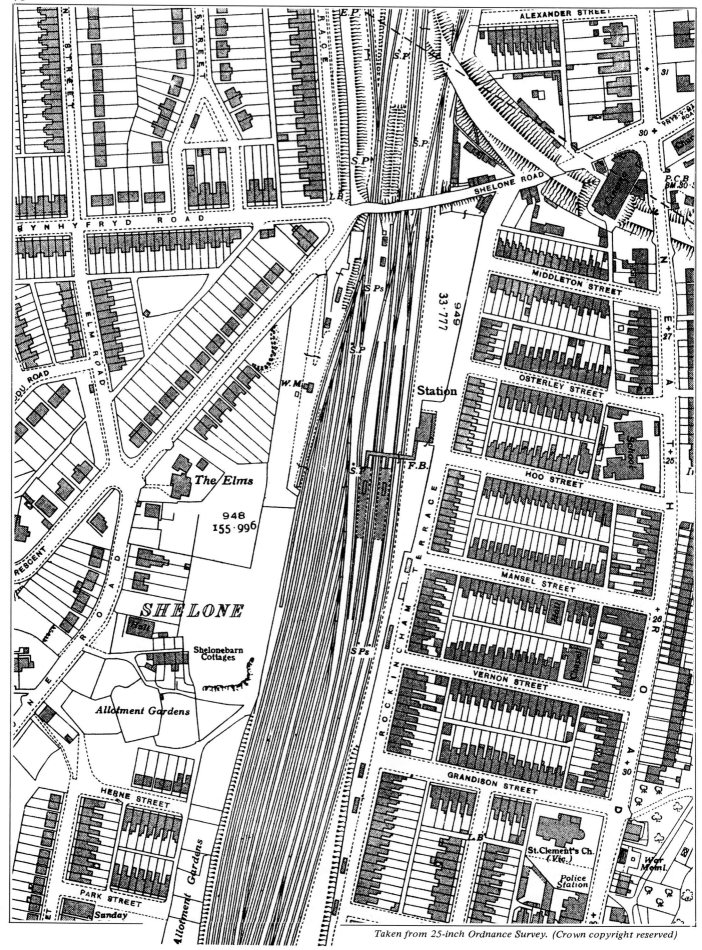

Taken from 25-inch Ordnance Survey. (Crown copyright reserved)

were divided at Baglan Junction, with down trains from the Aberavon direction joining the Down Relief by a direct line to the site of the old GWR station, whilst up trains left the Up Relief at the same point to pass beneath the Great Western lines, as before.

Also in 1935, the sidings to the west of the main lines and station were developed into a yard composed of six up and four down loop sidings, with the Up and Down Goods Lines running between them.

The new Briton Ferry box was located to the west of the old station site, well separated from the new four-track section by the goods running loops and another siding.

Briton Ferry station was closed in November 1964, and with the introduction of MAS in 1965, the signal box closed in March of that year.

The Down Relief line was taken out of use in March 1965, with slow trains using the Down Goods. The Up Avoiding Line went in November 1968. Track rationalisation continued in the 1980s: three of the up sidings in the yard went in 1981, and the up R & SB Avoiding Line, kept for egress from the Swansea Docks area, was cut back by 8 chains at the south end in July 1986 before joining the Up Main.

Briton Ferry station c. 1963, looking south from the Down Main platform towards Port Talbot. The 1935 design comprised two island platforms, each having waiting rooms, with the Mains through the centre and Reliefs against the outer faces. The main station building was to the east of the station (on the left in this view), beyond the Up Avoiding line, and next to the street, serving the platforms by means of the substantial footbridge. Water columns were provided at the departure end of each island, serving both Main and Relief lines. When this new station opened, the former R & SB Briton Ferry (East) station (alongside the old Great Western station) was soon closed, though initially R & SB trains still called there rather than at the new station.
LENS of SUTTON COLLECTION

Briton Ferry station on 27th June 1960, with Old Oak Common double-chimney 'Castle' No. 7036 *Taunton Castle* passing under the roadbridge with the 12.5 p.m. Milford Haven to Paddington (Train 'A11'; 2.30 p.m. ex-Swansea). The main expresses did not call at Briton Ferry, although the pedestrian 1.0 a.m. Paddington did, having become an all-stations train from Bridgend. The goods lines to the west of the station can be seen on the left, having passed through the centre of the sidings adjacent to the station.

Landore 'Hall' No. 5909 *Newton Hall* running through the Down Main platform at Briton Ferry with the 9.15 a.m Manchester (London Road) to Swansea on Monday, 27th June 1960. The up avoiding line may be seen in this view, on the left, passing by the main station building. The R & SB line ran independently on this side of the site until 1935. To the right, beyond the water tower, were a group of ten goods loop sidings, with the up and down goods lines passing through their centre.

COURT SART JUNCTION

Eleven days after being allocated to Landore from Bath Road, and some 8 months after heavy repair at Swindon, 'Castle' No. 5015 *Kingswear Castle* (as yet without the Landore shine) is seen with the eight-coach up 'South Wales Pullman' passing Court Sart box on Monday, 27th June 1960. The disused skew bridge on the right originally carried the South Wales Mineral Railway line from the North Rhondda Colliery, Glyncorrwg and Cymmer, passing over both the R & SB and the main line to join with the line to Swansea Docks near Neath Jct. (R & SB) box. A portion of the western half of the line was closed in the 1920s, although a connection from the west to Balls Yard (to the right of the bridge) was shown in situ until at least the 1940s.

In 1886, Neath Harbour Railways (authorised under the Neath Harbour Act 1874) completed a junction in the previously plain section of the main line between Briton Ferry and Neath, to take trains directly into Swansea Docks. However, this connection, named Neath Harbour Junction, was not brought into use, as the line beyond remained unbuilt.

Just to the south of the unused junction, the main line was crossed by an overbridge carrying the South Wales Mineral Railway from Tonmawr, which came to an end alongside the stubs of the NHR line, with an engine shed opened in 1877 (closed 1910) close by. To the north, in the angle formed by the GWR line and the nearby Neath Canal, the Great Western opened their own Neath engine shed.

Progress towards Swansea Docks occurred in 1894, when the R & SB line from their Briton Ferry station was opened for goods traffic (1895 for passenger); this extended line ran immediately to the east of the main line, and passed under the GWR line en route to Swansea just to the north of the unused Neath Harbour Junction. The R & SB had reached Briton Ferry from Treherbert and Aberavon in late 1893, and the new line to Swansea was an extension of that route, utilising part of the unbuilt NHT line, with a station at Court Sart, at a point just to the east of the bridge carrying the GWR line over it. With the building of the R & SB line, the

South Wales Mineral line had effected a connection into it at Neath Junction, directly behind the Neath engine shed.

The connecting line from the unused junction on the GWR to the R & SB line for Swansea was opened in 1903, when Neath Harbour Junction box was renamed Court Sart Junction. The junction with the R & SB was made at Neath Junction box, along with the SWM line.

In 1914, a new layout was installed at Court Sart, dispensing with the old 1886 Neath Harbour Junction. An Up flying loop was constructed from the R & SB line, avoiding Court Sart station, then running alongside the R & SB to join the Great Western route to the south of the South Wales Mineral overbridge. At the same time, a down loop was laid in from the down GWR main line, at around the site of the former double junction, running into the Down R & SB line. This, of course, removed the possibility of conflicting movements between Up R & SB and Down GWR Main line traffic. A new box, positioned nearer to the South Wales Mineral overbridge, was opened at the same time.

Further alterations were made in 1925 with the adjustment of the former South Wales Mineral line into Up and Down Goods lines, connecting with the flying loops by means of a double junction at Neath Junction.

Court Sart, with Landore '56XX' No. 5625 approaching Briton Ferry on Friday, 1st September 1961 at the head of a four-coach empty stock train, probably for Porthcawl. The signal placed the train on the relief line through the station.

The R & SB Court Sart station was closed in 1935, and the line serving it was taken out of use, leaving only the Up flying loop running to the east of the SWML, and the Down loop (with the Up & Down Goods lines) on the other side. However, two lines to the south of the former station were retained as sidings until 1964.

In 1961, a connecting line from Neath Engine Shed onto the Up Flying Loop was introduced, but this was taken out in March 1965, when Court Sart Junction box was also closed under the MAS scheme.

Another view of Court Sart Junction, seen on 27th August 1959. On the left are the connecting lines between the goods running and main lines, with 2–8–0T No. 4281 en route to Neath. The goods running lines for the R & SB route (of which the up line can be seen dropping down to the left of the engine to form its connection into Briton Ferry yard) continued at the higher level around the corner to join with the up and down 'flying loops' at Neath Jct. on the R & SB. The up 'flying loop' can be seen on the right at a lower level, having passed beneath the main lines in the distance (at the limit of visibility in this photograph). Court Sart (R & SB) station, closed in 1935, was located in the area behind and beyond the box. A busy passenger location, it had a terminating motor service from Neath (Canalside) and through trains between Swansea (Riverside, and after 1933, East Dock) and Treherbert. MICHAEL HALE

The view from the road bridge to the north of Briton Ferry station, with the up 'South Wales Pullman' approaching Briton Ferry on Friday, 1st September 1961, headed by Landore 'Castle' No. 5062 *Earl of Shaftesbury*, transferred to Landore from Bath Road in September 1960. She emerged from a Heavy Intermediate repair at Swindon in January 1961, and was eight months out of shops when this photograph was taken, but her appearance was still pristine, so typical of what was achieved day after day by Landore depot cleaners.

84

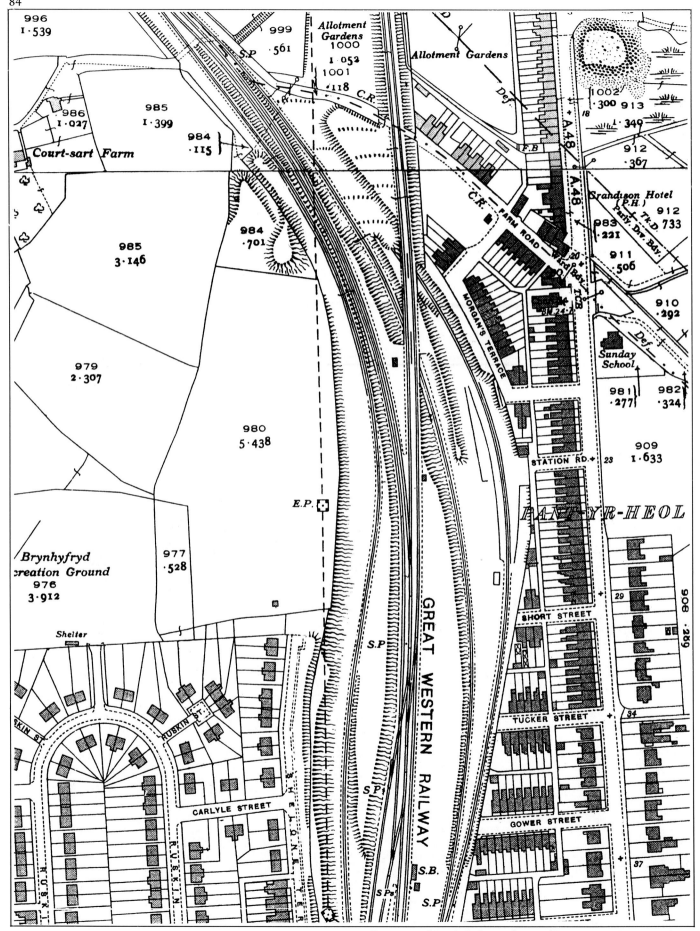

Neath '52XX' 2–8–oT No. 5222 on the R & SB line from Swansea Docks approaching Briton Ferry station with a train of empty mineral wagons en route to one of the collieries in the area on Thursday, 12th May 1960. The engine was taking the Up Avoiding line through the station area; the nearer line led to the Up Main and Relief.

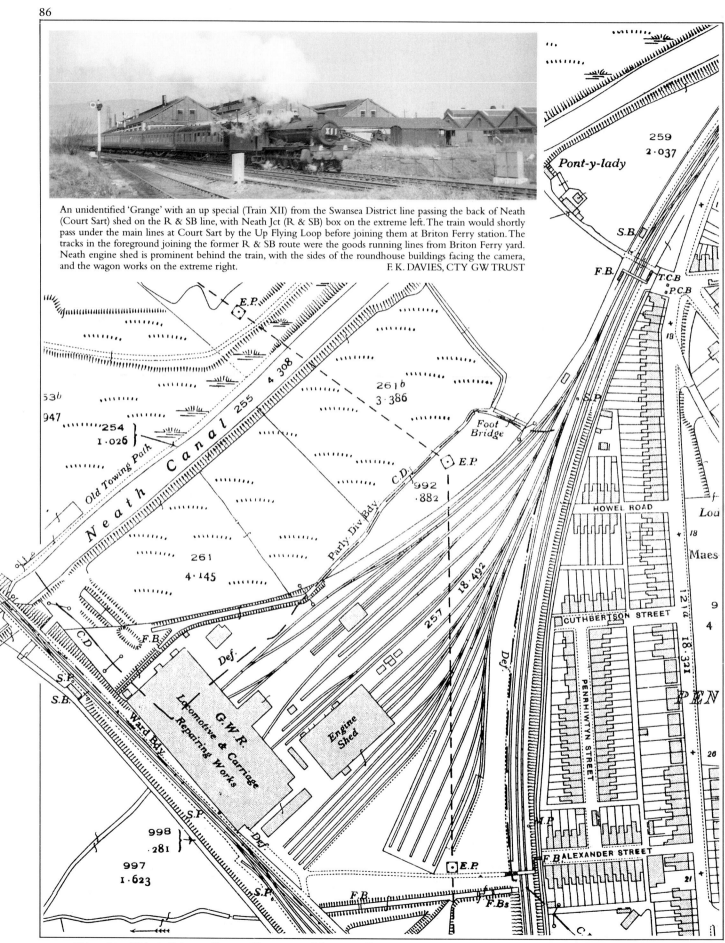

An unidentified 'Grange' with an up special (Train XII) from the Swansea District line passing the back of Neath (Court Sart) shed on the R & SB line, with Neath Jct (R & SB) box on the extreme left. The train would shortly pass under the main lines at Court Sart by the Up Flying Loop before joining them at Briton Ferry station. The tracks in the foreground joining the former R & SB route were the goods running lines from Briton Ferry yard. Neath engine shed is prominent behind the train, with the sides of the roundhouse buildings facing the camera, and the wagon works on the extreme right. F. K. DAVIES, CTY GW TRUST

Taken from 25-inch Ordnance Survey. (Crown copyright reserved)

NEATH (COURT SART) MPD

An atmospheric 1963 view of part of the shed yard, with a '42XX' under the coaling stage on the left, the coal tub's rail extension projecting out over its bunker. Neath's breakdown vehicles can be seen in the centre with a couple of wooden-bodied wagons, and an '84XX' on the right, standing on the short siding alongside the shed entrance road.
R. HOOPER, CTY DEAN FOREST RAILWAY SOCIETY

In 1862, an engine shed was opened at Neath by the Vale of Neath company, situated just to the south of the station on the east side of the running lines. This contained one through road with two dead end sidings, a turntable, and water and coaling facilities.

The GWR engine shed was opened in 1876 in a two-round-house style with in and out roads serving each, and a long road between, located at Court Sart within the vee of the main line to Neath and the R & SB line to Swansea Docks. With its opening, the old Vale of Neath shed was closed.

There was also a through siding laid in 1883 to carry materials for the building of the Neath Harbour Railway, but largely unused. Access to the shed from the main lines was by means of a lengthy road that ran parallel to the mains, with access at Neath No. 1 box, at Melincrythan Crossing, half-a-mile to the north.

Later access to the shed from the main line was at Neath Engine Shed box, opened in 1892, and a lot closer to the shed. There were connections to both mains at this point. At the same time, the northern part of the original shed access line became the Down Avoiding, with entry effected at the same box. The original Neath Engine Shed box was on the east side of the line, but was moved to the west side, probably in 1928.

By 1899 crossovers had been introduced between the tracks accessing the two roundhouses to create greater flexibility, and Carriage & Wagon Shops, fed by five sidings, with a further set of

five sidings for C&W use, had also been laid in to the east of the main shed.

Neath depot had important main-line commitments in the late Victorian and early Edwardian eras, when engines were changed at Neath on Paddington to West Wales services, with incoming Swindon-based 'Barnum' class 2-4-0s requiring servicing before their return journey, with two 'Stellas' based at Neath for their part of the workings. The most common engine type on the West Wales services to the west of Neath in the 1880s/90s was the '806' (Armstrong)/'2201' (Dean) class 2-4-0.

In January 1902, Neath had an allocation of 38 engines, made up of:

2	'3232' 2-4-0s
1	'Stella' 2-4-0
8	0-6-0s
1	'Aberdare' 2-6-0 (new)
2	'517' 0-4-2T (Nos. 571, 832)
24	Saddle/Pannier Tank 0-6-0s

The introduction of 'Atbara' 4-4-0s into the Paddington to South & West Wales workings in 1903 with the opening of the Badminton route, together with the presence of the water troughs at Goring and Chipping Sodbury, meant that engines were now capable of working through from London to Cardiff, and the pre-

A distant view of Neath shed taken on 22nd September 1962 from a passing train on the main line. The two turntables were accommodated in the three large sheds to the left, with the loco yard to their right, immediately behind the wagon repair shops, which are seen to the right. Wagon sidings associated with the repair shop are seen on its near side, with vehicles waiting attention.
R.S. CARPENTER

A 1963 view of the shed yard, showing the sidings on either side of the coaling stage, looking towards the roundhouses. The three tender engines on the right, including a '28XX' and a 'Grange', had been coaled and prepared for their next duty, whilst a '56XX' and a '28XX' can be seen on the siding alongside the entrance to the roundhouse. No. 8102 is seen in the centre with various tank engines on the other side of the coaling plant, well representative of the cross-section of engine types to be found at Neath at that time. The second entrance to this section of the shed is seen immediately to the right of the 2–6–2T.
H.B. PRIESTLEY, CTY P. READ

vious engine-changing basis of Paddington & Swindon, Swindon & Neath, and Neath & West Wales was replaced by Paddington & Cardiff and Cardiff & West Wales. This removed Neath from its role as a major engine changing point, and its allocation of express passenger engines developed no further until 1961 (qv).

Neath did retain an allocation of one or two Dukes from 1903 until 1910, but its main 4-4-0 allocation was of the mixed traffic 'Bulldogs', which lasted from 1904 to 1915, generally at a level of between three and five, but then fell away to only one (at most) until 1948. An unknown development appears to have occurred in 1915, when Neath received an 'Atbara' and a 'Badminton' 4-4-0, the former remaining until 1916, after which their only involvement with the 4-4-0 fleet was with 'Bulldogs'.

In 1913 coal stacking sidings were added on the east side of the shed yard, close to the main lines, whilst a new coal stage was provided from 1921 on the track between the two roundhouse feed roads.

Although Neath was the divisional shed, its known repair facilities were limited to light work. When heavier repair was required, Neath's engines tended to go to Caerphilly or Danygraig, with Swindon for major work.

During the 1920s and 30s, Neath was home to around six 2-8-0s, initially all of the 'ROD' type, but from 1931, also '28XXs'. There were a small number of '43XX' 2-6-0s also there during the 1920s

and early 30s. The allocation of '28XXs' reached seven in the early war years, but all were transferred away in 1942. From that time, '42XXs' became the dominant heavy engine.

During the 1950s, Neath Court Sart normally had an allocation of some 60 locomotives, until September 1961 (qv). Tank engines predominated, with only a few tender engines for main-line long-distance operations. At the end of 1953, the allocation stood at 63 engines, made up of:

2	'WD' 2-8-0s
15	'42XX' 2-8-0Ts
2	'51XX'
1	'81XX'
34	'57XX'
8	'84XX'
1	'16XX'

Of these, the '51XX' and '81XX' 2-6-2Ts were for use on the Vale of Neath, R&SB and Swansea services, the '42XXs' on main-line and local freight services and the two 'WDs' for main-line freight. The 'WDs' had replaced the Neath allocation of '2800' class 2-8-0s, which had ceased in 1942 after starting that year with six. There had never been a strong presence of this class at Neath until 1939, the previous level being mostly one between 1913–32, rising then from 1933–38 from two to four, before achieving a peak of

Standing on a coal stage road awaiting its turn for servicing, Tondu (88H) 2–8–0T No. 5243 had probably worked into Neath with a Control duty. Six or seven of that shed's '42s' worked to Margam daily, but none was regularly scheduled beyond. The piles of clinker on the ground do not suggest a yard kept particularly tidy at this late stage of steam operation, on 5th July 1963.
D. K. JONES

A very grimy Neath '43XX' Mogul No. 7312 pulling forward from the coaling stage to go straight off shed in September 1963. The coal stage was accessible from both sides, with each road running beyond, straight onto the appropriate turntable.
ROGER HOLMES. CTY. HUGH DAVIES

Neath '42XX' No. 4282 at Court Sart depot in the mid-1950s. This engine was transferred from Severn Tunnel Jct. to Neath in May 1953, and remained there into the 'sixties. Soon after its arrival, Neath's allocation of these engines stood at 15, with 12 turns specified; the '42s' were mainly used for local duties, and were usually only seen on through freights for English destinations as far as Cardiff or Severn Tunnel Jct., where they were handed over to 2–8–0s.
LENS OF SUTTON

eight in 1940. The class disappeared completely from Neath between 1943 and 1962, by which time there was a huge surplus of power, though in poor condition. Three '28s' were allocated at the end of 1962, rising to seven in 1963, all being removed when the depot closed in June 1965.

Only one 'Hall' was ever allocated to Neath until 1960, this being No. 4934 between October 1932 and January 1934. Following the introduction of main-line diesel power in the West of England, five 'Halls' were allocated to Neath in June 1960, with another in October, presumably for newly-allocated duties connected with Margam Yard. However, their presence was short-lived even with the arrival of four more with the closure of Landore in June1961, as by the end of that year only three 'Halls' survived at the depot. Five new 'Halls' arrived during 1962 but five were also transferred away, still leaving three at the end of the year, which became two by the end of 1963, all going by the end of 1964 at depot closure.

With the closure of Landore in the summer of 1961 for conversion to a diesel depot, Neath (Court Sart) took over the Landore allocation of main-line passenger engines for working east of Swansea, and from June/July a total of twelve 'Castles' were allocated, mostly for working the four top-link overnight turns to London, which accounted for eight engines.

The coal stacking sidings were taken out in 1961 with a new connection made through the site to enable engines to leave the shed and join the Up Flying Loop, although this was taken out again in March 1965. The shed closed in June 1965, although the sidings remained in use until August 1966, and the Wagon Repair Shops until February 1968.

Neath (Court Sart) was the parent depot of the Neath Division, which extended from Duffryn Yard to Fishguard. It was coded 'NEA' by the Great Western, and became '87A' from 1948.

2–8–0T No. 4264 stabled in the roundhouse on 25th August 1959. At this time, the '42s' were by far the most numerous main-line type at the shed, which had thirteen of them to work ten freight diagrams. Some ran to and from Aberdare, Llandilo Jct., Newport and Severn Tunnel whilst others were scheduled to take trains for English destinations as far as Cardiff.
F. A. BLENCOWE,
CTY. R. K. BLENCOWE

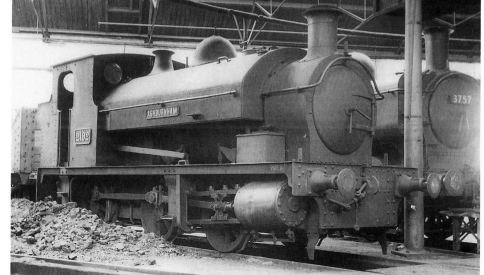

Ex-Barry Port & Gwendraeth Valley 0–6–6T No. 2192 *Ashburnam*, which shunted the dock lines at Neath, is seen here in the roundhouse next to local pannier No. 3757, on 9th February 1950. It was much sought-after by enthusiasts at this time and was withdrawn in April 1951.
G. F. DOUGLAS CTY. R. K. BLENCOWE

An interior view of Neath roundhouse in September 1963, showing a good cross-section of the type of engines to be found at the depot at that time, with '57XX', '41XX' (No. 4108), '43XX' (No. 7318), '28XX' and '42XX' (No. 5241) engines evident. There were 24 roads off each table, two of which led to the outside, and a third connecting with the other table. Neath '28XXs' were scheduled for the daily Yarnton train at this time.
ROGER HOLMES, CTY. HUGH DAVIES

A section of the Neath roundhouse on 25th August 1959, showing 2–8–0T No. 4242 with sister engine and two pannier tanks, and part of the turntable itself with under-rigging. The two parts of the shed, each served by separate turntables, were specified as passenger and freight in earlier years, although by the end of steam little differentiation was probably necessary.

F. A. BLENCOWE,
CTY. R. K. BLENCOWE

A visiting '84XX' – No. 8444 of Aberdare – and pannier No. 7701 in the roundhouse on 25th August 1959. The '84' would probably work a Vale of Neath service back to Aberdare.

F. A. BLENCOWE,
CTY. R. K. BLENCOWE

Allocated for working passenger services on the Vale of Neath line to Pontypool Road, the sole Neath-based 2–6–2T '41XX' No. 4169 is seen in the roundhouse on 28th February 1954. This class of engine was much in demand at depots all over the region, though it was poorly represented in the Neath Division, with only odd examples at Neath itself, Landore, Carmarthen and Whitland.

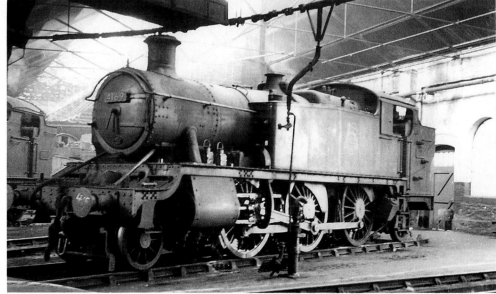

It was a sad sight to see the large number of condemned engines standing at such depots as Neath, awaiting removal to scrap-metal merchants for cutting up. By September 1963, engines for disposal were becoming increasingly common. 2–8–0 No. 2857 had a happy ending, being one of the engines bought by David Woodham. She languished at Barry from 1963 until 1974, when bought by the 2857 Society and was restored on the Severn Valley Railway. The engine is seen here at Neath in September 1963.

ROGER HOLMES,
CTY. HUGH DAVIES

Neath-based Mogul No. 7320 standing at the throat of the depot, with the main lines on the extreme right, probably on its way out of the depot on 5th July 1963. It is devoid of a tail lamp except for an unofficial one placed on the right-hand frame. The nearer track was used by inwards engines on their way to the servicing road for firedropping and coaling.   D.K. JONES

NEATH GENERAL

The southern approaches to Neath station, seen from an overbridge looking north on 6th June 1963, with the two main lines on the right, and Neath East box just off the picture, to the right of the photographer. The '56XX' running along the Up Main with a short coal train was probably heading for Margam, with the Wales & Monmouth Industrial Estate to its right; this site had its own private line running along the front of the buildings, behind the wall. The '84XX' hauled train on the Down Goods line may have been a Margam to Neath Goods, perhaps servicing some of the remaining private sidings in the area. In the middle distance, beyond the '84', the goods lines became Up and Down, as the main and goods lines swung away from each other to accommodate the nests of Up and Down marshalling sidings between them. The goods shed may be seen in the far distance, ahead of the '84XX'.
R. H. MARROWS

The main line follows a north-easterly course from Court Sart, through Neath station to the junction with the Vale of Neath line, where it swings round to resume the general east-west direction abandoned to the west of Pyle.

Neath passenger station underwent a considerable number of changes in its history, not only in design but also in location. The first Neath station, opened in June 1850 by the South Wales Railway, was located on the north-western outskirts of the town, the site of the ultimate Neath General station. From September 1851, it also handled traffic from the newly-opened Vale of Neath Railway, which had been completed from Aberdare, and joined the SWR by a junction just to the north of the station. The first station eventually comprised a main island platform with two outer, smaller platforms. There was also a small goods shed where the ultimate goods building would be, to the south-west of the station. An engine shed with turntable stood to the south of the station, alongside and to the east of the main lines. Another goods shed stood to the east of this, possibly of Vale of Neath origin, with several sidings around it, probably for the marshalling of up trains, perhaps formed of wagons from the Vale of Neath line.

This first passenger station was closed in 1865, and was replaced by a new station on the bridge over the Vale of Neath/Swansea & Neath line into Swansea Docks, just over a quarter-of-a-mile to the north. The second station was a simple design, comprised of up and down main platforms only, located beyond the junction with the Vale of Neath line, and adjacent to the new 1863 Low Level (later, Bridge St., then Riverside) station on the VoN/S & N line. This

new position doubtless had interchange in mind, as the Neath & Brecon Railway also arrived on the scene at Low Level in 1864. The Vale of Neath was absorbed into the Great Western in 1865, and soon afterwards the passenger trains from that line once more used the main-line route into Swansea, calling at 'Neath Old' station to reverse.

The second station was closed in 1877, and a new station, composed of up and down platforms only with a through siding line between, was built on the original site, opening in June 1877. The new engine shed at Court Sart had been opened in 1876, so the original shed on the east side of the running lines was removed and those lines slewed eastwards to enable a freight yard to be created between them and the Up and Down Goods lines on the west side of the site. Four sidings, stop-blocked at the north end, provided for eastbound traffic, whilst five sidings stop-blocked at their south end were used for westwards and Vale of Neath departures. The main goods shed to the south-west of the station was considerably enlarged, but the shed on the east side of the site was removed, the area becoming a permanent way yard. The number of signal boxes was reduced, with No. 1 still being at the south end of the complex (though now placed on the east side of the running lines), whilst the original No. 2 controlling access to the sidings on the east side was taken out, as was No. 3 at the north end of the main passenger platform. A new No. 2 box was opened at the south end of the Down platform. A private siding for Neath Gas Works was also opened on the south side in 1877.

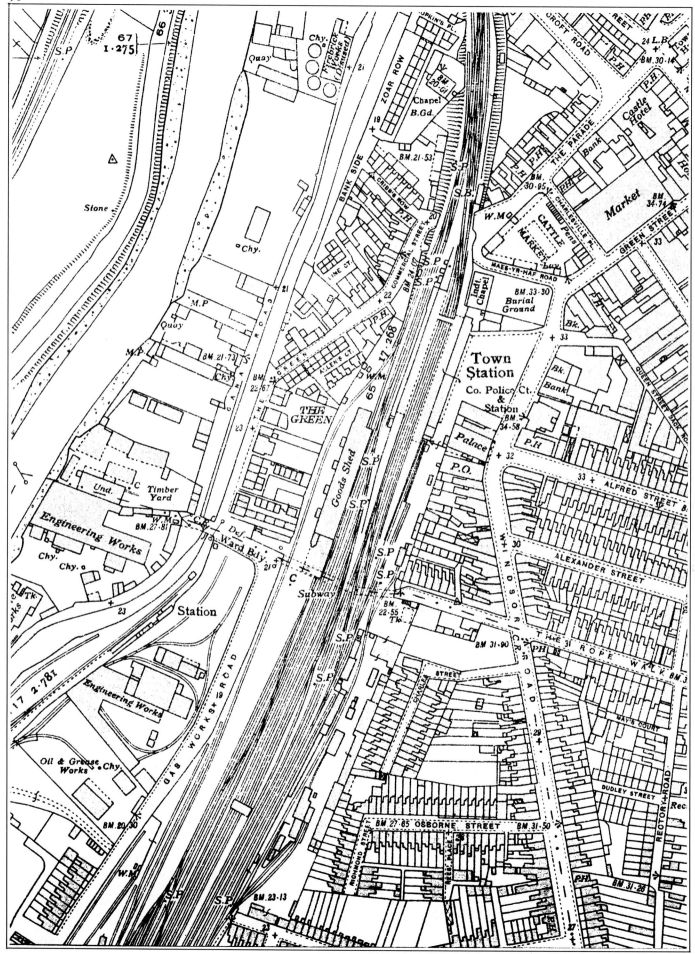

Taken from 25-inch Ordnance Survey. (Crown copyright reserved)

Neath station played a significant role in the working of London & West Wales services in the later Victorian years and early Edwardian era. These trains changed engines at Neath, the incoming Swindon-based '69' class 2-2-2s, then '806/2201' class 2-4-0s and 'Barnum' 2-4-0s, being replaced by Neath, Carmarthen Junction or New Milford '806/2201' class 2-4-0s, or occasionally 0-6-0s, which worked forward to destination; a reverse arrangement existed in the up direction.

By January 1901, Neath depot had two '2201s' and a 'Stella' for its main passenger duties, whilst New Milford and Carmarthen Junction depots each had five '2201s', with thirty 'Standard Goods' 0-6-0s shared between the three sheds; these engines would have been very familiar sights at the station's platforms. Main-line engine changing at Neath station ceased in 1903, when London & West Wales services, now worked by more powerful 4-4-0s, changed engines at Cardiff, setting the scene for future years.

Landore 'Castle' No. 7028 *Cadbury Castle* with the down 'Pembroke Coast Express' running non-stop through Neath General on Monday, 27th June 1960, and photographed from the south end of the down platform. The siding on the extreme right was part of four sidings stop-blocked at their southern end, which were used to hold various traffics, including the District Civil Engineer's inspection coach, which can be seen beyond the wagon. Two through goods lines, running from East box (some 600 yards away), were provided to the right of these.

Neath 0–6–0PT No. 9430 shunting on the sidings to the south-west of the station on 21st March 1951, recorded from the southern end of the down platform. The Up and Down through goods lines that ran between the down station platform and the goods shed can be seen between the engine and the building.
F. K. DAVIES, CTY GW TRUST

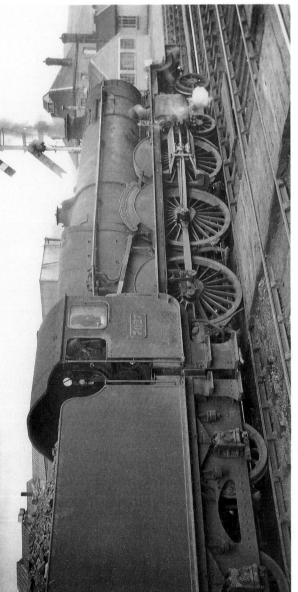

In the early post-Nationalisation era, Old Oak Common 'Castles' were probably not as well looked after as they had been in the interwar period, due mostly to the postwar manpower shortages; No. 7027 *Thornbury Castle*, in a far from pristine condition, is seen here at the head of a London service on Saturday, 4th August 1951. Entering traffic in August 1949, the engine was due for its first Heavy Intermediate repair, and was sent to Swindon factory three weeks after this photograph was taken. Given the imminence of that visit, perhaps the Old Oak cleaners were directed at more appropriate work.
F.K. DAVIES, CTY GW TRUST

Aberdare '56XX' No. 5647 standing in the middle road at Neath General with the empty stock for a late-morning return Vale of Neath service in 1963. The three coaches were corridor vehicles, as was normal for VoN services, the second coach being London Midland stock. The well-cleaned condition of the engine was typical of the turn-out by Aberdare shed, which was one of the best in the Valleys for presentation. Engineers' coach, No. WD150328, on the left was standing in the up bay, there being a Permanent Way Engineer's depot just outside the station on the up side.
R. HOOPER,
CTY DEAN FOREST
RAILWAY SOCIETY

In 1896, the platforms were extended and a new Up bay platform provided at the south end of the Up platform, with cattle pens added. Around 1898, the signal boxes were renamed Neath East and Neath Centre.

By 1913, the goods depot had become a thriving concern and further yard sidings were added for full load traffic.

The station was renamed Neath General in 1924, and in 1926 the Neath Centre box became Neath General Middle.

The Down platform was lengthened in 1958. In 1959, the double Junction at Neath East – where the goods lines converged into the mains to the south of the station – was replaced by a slip and a crossover arrangement.

In 1965, the goods shed was closed; 'smalls' traffic was then handled from Swansea Goods, and full loads from Hafod Yard. The goods yard sidings were recovered, along with most of the stop-blocked sidings to its north. Following the closure of the Vale of Neath as a through route in 1965, the connection from the station onto that line at Neath Junction was removed in 1966.

By 1972, virtually all the remaining sidings around the station had been recovered, leaving only the Up and Down main. Neath East box became Neath from October 1967, as MAS was introduced to the west. In 1973, the box was reduced to a ground frame, and this was removed in 1977.

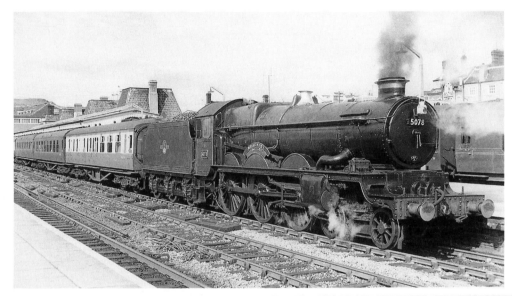

Neath General station, with Neath 'Castle' No. 5078 *Beaufort* standing at the up platform with a stopping service, probably for Gloucester, on Saturday, 30th June 1962. The engine had been moved from Landore to Neath in September 1961 with the closure of Landore for conversion to a diesel depot. The centre road through Neath station was originally part of a very lengthy siding with trailing connections to each main, running on for ¼-mile to the south of the station; by this time, it had been split into two around its half-way mark. An up bay was provided at the south end of the up platform, seen behind the engine.

F. K. DAVIES, CTY GW TRUST

Neath's Standard 'Class 4' 2–6–4T No. 80133 alongside the up platform at Neath around 1 o'clock with the 10.55 a.m. Vale of Neath service from Pontypool Road, whilst the 8.55 a.m. Paddington to Pembroke Dock service was occupying the down platform. The 'Class 4s' were allocated to the area in 1963 for local services, with one at Neath and two at Swansea East Dock. An earnest conversation was taking place between a group of gangers on the middle road. The Civil Engineer's Inspection coach on the right was standing in the up bay platform.

R. H. MARROWS

Newport '51XX' 2–6–2 tank No. 4145 easing into the up platform at Neath with its four-coach set on a Vale of Neath service on Saturday 9th May 1953. The well-patronised up platform (No. 1) suggests that a London service could well have been following, while a down service for Swansea was departing from platform No. 2.

T. J. EDGINGTON

Neath General station, viewed from the 'west' end (actually facing south at this point), showing the up platform on the left on 9th September 1951. The main line can be seen snaking its way through the station and the goods yard on the far side. The connection in the foreground linked the two main lines, whilst the through line in the centre can be seen feeding into the down main line near the end of the platform.   H. C. CASSERLEY

The heart of the station is shown in this picture of a Swansea to Treherbert train standing at the up platform behind Treherbert 0–6–2T No. 5667 on 1st December 1962, the train composed of a 5-coach 'Valleys' set. These services took the South Wales main line route through Neath and Briton Ferry, then the R & SB route at Briton Ferry box, to run via Baglan Jct. for Aberavon Town, Cymmer Afan and Treherbert. The centre road was utilised for holding empty stock. Again, the buildings were of local stone, with beige dressing stones to the corners and apertures.

F. K. DAVIES, CTY GW TRUST

Neath '94XX' 0–6–0PT No. 9452 had backed onto a Vale of Neath service on Saturday, 1st December 1962; this was a Pontypool Road to Swansea train, working forward from Neath General (where the train reversed) for the twenty-minute journey to High Street station. Some of these services commenced or terminated at Neath, but those to or from Swansea were allowed five or more minutes for the reversing procedure. The coaching stock by this time was scheduled as three- or four-coach corridor sets.

F. K. DAVIES, CTY GW TRUST

Cardiff East Dock 'Castle' No. 5081 *Lockheed Hudson* is seen here alongside the down platform with a relief service for Swansea on Thursday, 6th June 1963. The underslung signals at the departure end of the down platform, so positioned to be seen under the station footbridge from an approaching engine, are illustrated to good effect here. The days of the Cardiff 'shine' on their allocated 'Castles' had long gone by this time and No. 5081 only had another 4 months to go before withdrawal.

R. H. MARROWS

The 'west' end of the station (facing north from the up platform at this point), looking towards the Vale of Neath junction and the main line on to Skewen. The goods lines ran behind the station on the extreme left, whilst in front the underhung down line splitting signals for main line and Vale of Neath routes can be seen on the down platform. Neath General West box, seen ahead, replaced Neath West box (located nearer the Vale of Neath junction) in 1929, being itself closed under MAS in 1967. 'Manor' Class 4-6-0 No. 7829 *Ramsbury Manor* of Carmarthen depot is seen arriving with the 11.0 a.m. Vale of Neath service from Pontypool Road on 9th September 1951, due at 12.57 p.m., having called at eighteen intermediate stations on the way. With the closure of the Vale of Neath as a through route in 1965, the layout at the west end of Neath station was progressively simplified with impending MAS to become two main lines only, the goods lines being taken out in October 1965.

H. C. CASSERLEY

The view at the west end of Neath General (actually facing north at this point), with a '56XX' waiting for the signal on the middle road through the station. Neath West box is seen at the north end of the up platform, with the exit from the goods lines opposite, on the left. The Vale of Neath line split from the main line where the signals can be seen in the distance.

R. H. MARROWS

A September 1953 view, looking north along the main lines from Neath General towards Swansea, showing the Vale of Neath line feeding in from ahead in the distance, with the goods lines entering from behind the platform on the left; in between, the main line continued its curve around to the left for Swansea and West Wales. At the north end of the platforms, the goods lines joined into the mains by a double junction, whilst the Vale of Neath route diverged from the mains to the right by a similar arrangement (foreground). In the middle distance can be seen another double junction between the main and Vale of Neath lines, giving access to the latter from the goods lines (and vice versa).

P.J. GARLAND

From Court Sart to Neath, the South Wales main line was orientated generally south-west/north-east, though the signal boxes were named East and West, relating to the overall direction of travel between Paddington and Fishguard. Thus, the box at the north-eastern end of the station was named Neath West, featured in this picture as the 11.10 a.m. Milford Haven to Paddington (Train A90, 1.30 p.m. ex-Swansea) made its way down the bank into Neath General behind Old Oak Common 'Castle' No. 5056 *Earl of Powis* on Monday, 27th June 1960. No. 5056 was known to be one of the best-performing 'Castles' based at the London depot. The tracks on the left were originally the two goods running lines, though subsequently they were downgraded into connections from the down side yard, and were removed in October 1965.

An o–6–oPT banking a westbound freight train over the River Neath bridge on the main-line route, probably viewed from the A48 road bridge. The train's load appears to have been loaded mineral wagons, which the pannier tank would assist up the two-and-a-half miles of 1 in 99 and 1 in 88 gradients to Skewen summit. A '42XX', for example, could take 40 loaded coal up this gradient, but with a pannier assisting to Skewen the load could be increased to 65.   H. C. CASSERLEY

The two railway viaducts over the River Neath are seen this picture of 6th June 1963. The main-line bridgework carried on twin pillars features in the foreground, whilst the Vale of Neath on sets of triple pillars can be seen in the background. In 1905, the original Brunel timber-built main-line viaduct was replaced by the structure seen here. Although the Tennant Canal passed under the main-line viaduct with the river (to the left in this view), it did not curve around with the river to pass under the Vale of Neath viaduct. The river was at a low ebb when the picture was taken.
R.H. MARROWS

A July 1963 picture of the track layout to the north of Neath General, where the Vale of Neath line diverges to the right away from the main line, which itself swings around to the left from its north-easterly trajectory through Neath to once again assume a westerly alignment. Both lines crossed over the A48 trunk road by the bridge in the immediate foreground, then over Neath Canal beyond, the bridgework for which may be seen in the angle of the diverging routes. Further around the main line to the left may be seen the 80-yard Neath Viaduct, where the railway crossed over the River Neath and the Tennant Canal. From 1877, there were double junctions in both directions at this point between the two routes, but these were replaced by single connections from 1960. The bracket signal on the Up Main line carried the Neath General West box homes, which covered movements along the Up main, and also through the connection to the down platform.   P. J. GARLAND

On leaving Neath station, the main line curved around to the left from its north-easterly.heading to almost south-west. Here, a Neath to Brecon train is seen in Neath (Riverside) station while a main-line service crossed the bridge about halfway around that curve, en route from Neath General to Swansea, on Saturday, 14th July 1956. In 1865, the second of Neath's main-line stations to be built was located on the embankment across the site of this bridge, giving convenient interchange between the two routes. It was replaced by a third on the current site in the late 1870s.   T. J. EDGINGTON

The old Vale of Neath route between Pontypool and Neath is seen again here, with a '57XX' and van waiting at the north end of Neath Riverside platforms for the road on 6th June 1963. Neath Riverside box is shown at the end of the up platform, against the main-line overbridge, with the junction for the Neath & Brecon line a short distance beyond. The River Neath was just off to the right in this view.   R. H. MARROWS

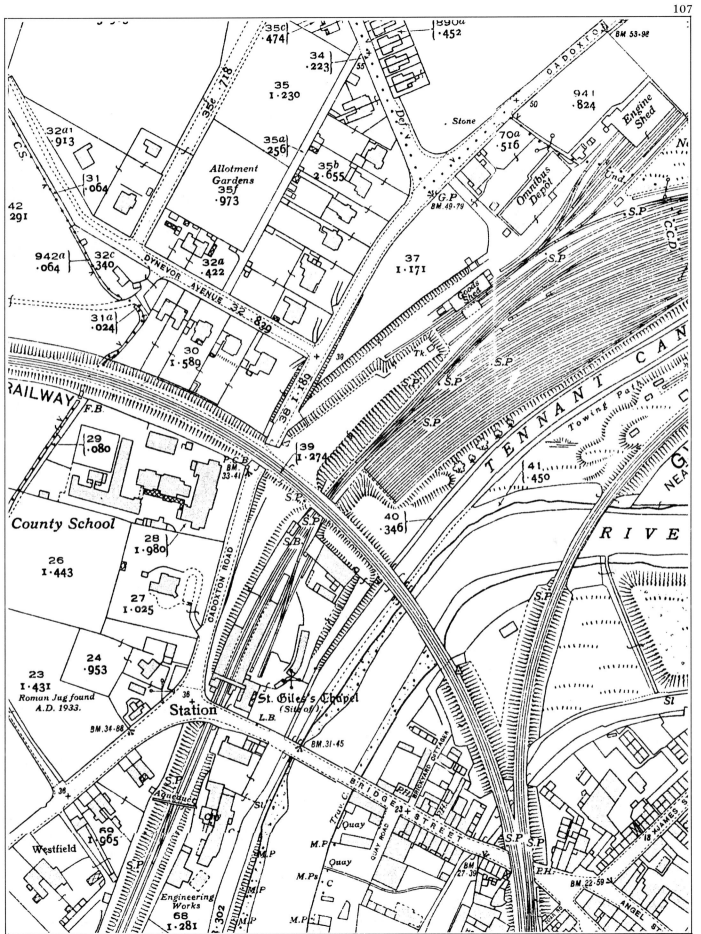

Taken from 25-inch Ordnance Survey. (Crown copyright reserved)

Skewen Station on 23rd September 1963, looking east. This was the second station to serve the village, and was built in 1910, replacing the first which was some quarter-mile to the west of this location. Only passenger and parcels facilities were available at this station, but goods and livestock were handled at the yard beyond the site of the old station; built in 1922, the yard was provided with a small goods shed, mileage sidings and a crane.

P. J. GARLAND

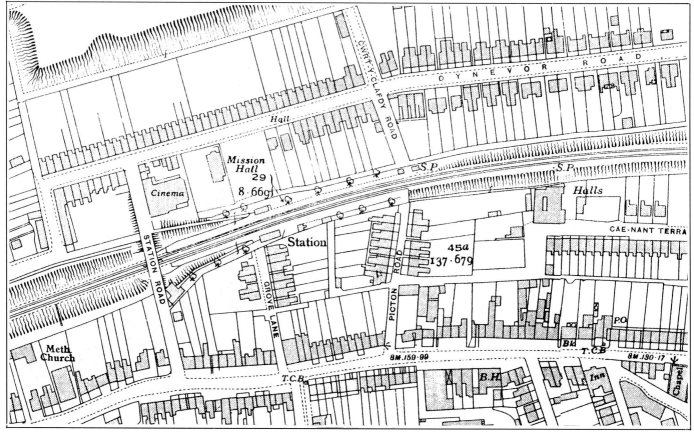

Taken from 25-inch Ordnance Survey for 1940. (Crown copyright reserved)

SKEWEN

The two intermediate stations between Neath and Landore were both subject to moves as the railway circumstances changed in the area.

In 1874, the main line running alongside Skewen village was double track, although two loop sidings on the north side of the Up line, known as East Llansamlet Sidings, were in use just beyond the western outskirts of the village. No passenger facilities were provided at this time, and travellers would mostly have used Llansamlet station, then a mile or so to the west.

In about 1880, a passenger station named Dynevor was opened just to the east of East Llansamlet Sidings, on the western edge of Skewen village, with up and down platforms only.

The site of the sidings was soon renamed Dynevor Sidings, and expansion of facilities took place. Dynevor Colliery Sidings were sited on the north side of the line by 1880, with access by a tramroad to Brithdir, Cwmdu, and Graigola Merthyr Collieries. Other sidings were developed on the south side of the line.

Dynevor station was renamed Skewen in October 1904.

By 1906, further expansion of sidings on both sides of the line had taken place to handle traffic in and out of the collieries, whilst up and down goods loops had been provided to the west, the eastern ends of which were controlled from Dynevor Sidings box, which was renewed in 1906. Skewen West box, opened in 1906, controlled the western end of the Goods loops.

In May 1910, a new passenger station was opened a quarter-mile further east, at a position rather more convenient for the village, and the old station was closed; again, the new station was comprised of Up and Down platforms only.

This also heralded work on the new Swansea District line, the junction for which was located at the site of the old station. The easterly section of the District line was opened from Skewen Junction as far as Felin Fran in February 1912, and onwards towards Llanelly during the following year. The junction was controlled by a new box, Skewen East, which was located in the 'V' between the two routes. Running concurrently with this work, the two goods loops had been extended eastwards to Skewen East box in 1911. Dynevor Sidings box was renamed around this time to Skewen Middle.

The colliery sidings at Dynevor/Middle box had been partially taken over by the GWR around the turn of the century for their own use, and in 1922 a new goods shed, with crane and a mileage siding, was opened at Skewen.

Skewen West box was closed in 1946, and Skewen Middle was renamed West at this time. The two goods running loops nevertheless remained in operation.

Most of these sidings fell into disuse with the closure of the collieries and works, and most were removed by the introduction of MAS in 1964, when Skewen West box was closed. The station was closed in November 1964 for passengers, and in September 1965 for goods traffic.

The section of the Swansea District line from Lonlas Jct. to Skewen East was closed to traffic in October 1965, by which time the last of the sidings had been taken out of use. The remains of the Up goods loop, running as far as Skewen East box was removed in 1966, though the box itself lasted until October 1973. Only the two main lines remain.

Skewen station, looking west along the main lines from the down platform, with the steel bridge carrying a small road over the railway at the far end of the platforms. Under the span of the bridge, in the distance, may be seen the bridge taking the A48 trunk road over the main lines, beyond which was Skewen East box and the site of the old station. There is no hint in this view of the industrial complex which lay beyond.

LENS of SUTTON

SKEWEN EAST JUNCTION

Passing the junction with the Swansea District Line at Skewen East, Canton Castle No. 5073 *Blenheim* is seen at the head of service 'T03', the 8.15 a.m. Swansea to Cardiff which on this Summer Saturday in 1961 appears to have been extended as a complete train to Paddington, departing Cardiff 9.45 a.m. At Cardiff, the oncoming engine would carry 1A32. Normally, the 8.15 a.m. ex-Swansea conveyed coaches to be attached to the up Red Dragon at Cardiff, which ran non-stop between Swansea and Cardiff.

HUW DANIEL

Crossing the junction with the Swansea District Line at Skewen East, Landore 'Castle' No. 4093 *Dunster Castle*, was returning home with the 10.55 a.m. Paddington to Pembroke Dock, though without the 'Pembroke Coast Express' headboard on this particular Saturday during the summer of 1959. The overbridge carrying the A48 across the railway forms the backdrop in this view. No. 4093 was a long-term Landore 'Castle', transferred there in October 1952, remaining in the area until early 1963 when she was finally moved to end her days at Bristol and Gloucester before finally succumbing at John Cashmore, Newport Dock in September 1964.   HUW DANIEL

Skewen East Jct., looking westwards, with Skewen East box within the divergence of the Swansea District line (left) and the old main line (right). The old route to Llanelly (via Landore) was a little over a mile shorter, but the District line avoided the congestion around Swansea, and the gradients of Cockett bank, beyond Landore. Skewen East was just 5½ miles from High Street.

Running eastwards along the final stretch of the Swansea District Line between Lonlas Jct. and Skewen East, Canton 'Castle' No. 5061 *Earl of Birkenhead* was heading the 8.48 a.m. Fishguard Harbour to Paddington Parcels and Empty Vans on Saturday 2nd June 1962. She had taken over the train at Felin Fran, and would work back to Cardiff, where a Gloucester 'Castle' or 'Hall' would take over as far as Swindon. Regular passenger-rated traffic over the District Line was light, with only a few parcels trains using it daily, together with one or two expresses – mostly Fishguard trains – that were not required to call at Swansea. Excursions did, however, use the route, particularly rugby specials from Llanelly and beyond. Skewen West box can be seen on the higher level main line; this box was opened as Dynevor Sidings in 1906 and renamed Skewen West in 1946, being closed under MAS in September 1964, together with Skewen Up Sidings, in which can be seen both passenger (an overflow from Maliphant) and freight stock on this day.   HUW DANIEL

Old Oak Common 'Castle' No. 4075 *Cardiff Castle* had a good head of steam – even though leaking from the front end – as she approached the road bridge near Lonlas, at the west end of Skewen Up Sidings and Mileage Yard. Her train was 'A11', the 12.5 p.m. Milford Haven to Paddington (2.30 p.m. ex-Swansea), which on weekdays also carried through coaches from Pembroke Dock, though on Saturdays conveyed only the Milford section, plus the usual dining car section from Swansea. Curiously, *Cardiff Castle* was only ever allocated to Cardiff Canton for some 8 months, between November 1931 and July 1932. Until 1946, Skewen West box was located around the corner, at the end of the goods loops; its name and the remaining functions were taken over by Dynevor Sidings box in that year.
HUW DANIEL

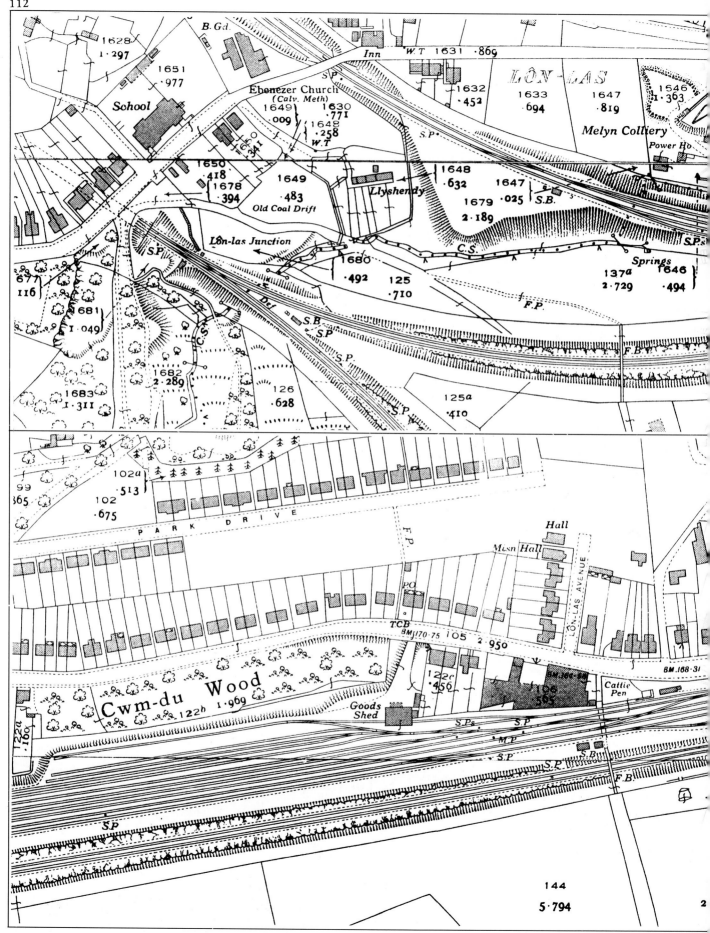

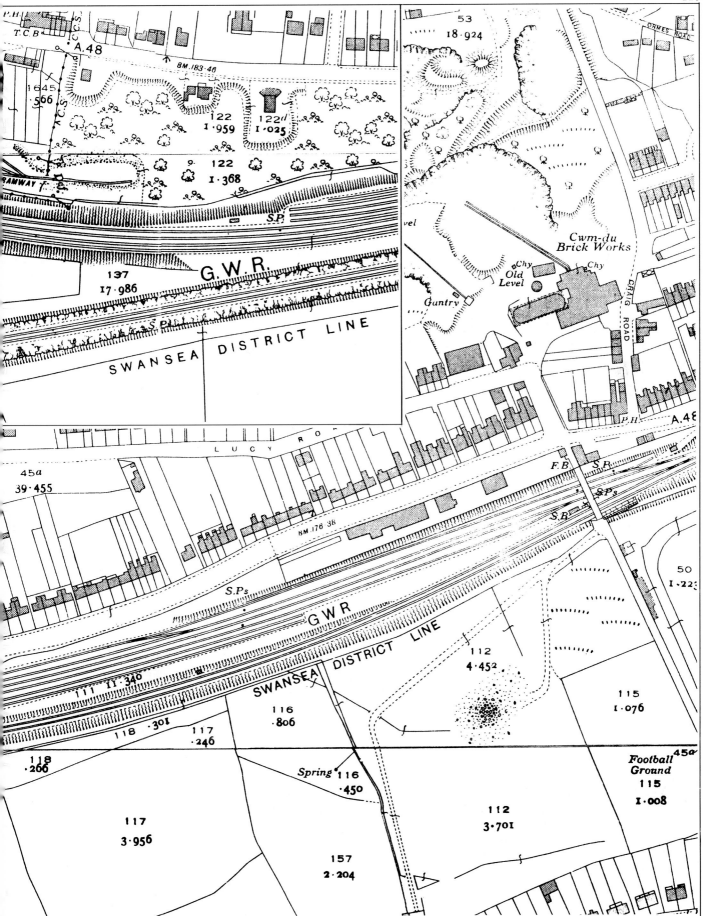

LLANSAMLET

The original Llansamlet station was sited less than a mile to the west of Dynevor (later, Skewen) station, near to the village of Lonlas. This station closed in January 1885, and a new station was opened a mile to the west, again comprising just two platforms. Within this distance was the site of the famous Brunel 'Flying Arches', four of which were constructed to maintain the banks of the cutting.

Between Skewen and Llansamlet, the GWR main line crossed over the Swansea District line, which at that point was within the 924-yard Lonlas tunnel, while near the new Llansamlet station, the Midland Railway's Swansea Vale line ran to the north, originally serving Samlet Colliery, and further west a hive of industrial concerns.

Llansamlet station, on 23rd September 1963. This was a replacement for the original station which was situated a mile to its east. As with the replacement station at Skewen, Llansamlet handled only passenger and parcel traffic, with goods being conveyed by East Skewen yard. As may be seen, the station was not provided with a footbridge between platforms, and passengers were enjoined to use the ramps running down from each platform to the road that passed beneath the railway.
P. J. GARLAND

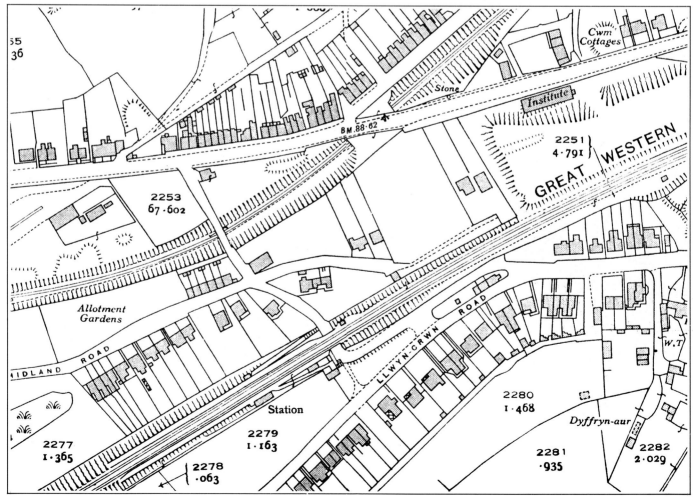

Taken from 25-inch Ordnance Survey for 1948. (Crown copyright reserved)

In February 1950, Llansamlet station was renamed 'Llansamlet North' to differentiate from the station on the Midland line, and remained so until replaced by a third station in recent years.

At Swansea Valley Junction (which should actually have been Swansea Vale Junction), there were connections from both sides of the main line with the sidings on the Swansea Vale Railway. Just below Six Pit Junction (on the Midland's Swansea Vale line) was the original point where the South Wales railway crossed the Swansea Vale line on the flat, but this was soon rebuilt so that the Swansea Vale ran under the South Wales main line. The connection on the northern side of the main lines, to Six Pit Jct. box, also contained the former transfer shed between the two companies. The ex-Midland line was closed to passenger services in 1875, which were thereafter routed by a new line via Morriston and Clydach.

By the early 1900s, there was considerable industrial activity at this location, with the Glamorgan Spelter Co., Foxholes Colliery and Llansamlet Spelter Works all on the north side of the line.

A Down Goods Loop was brought into use from 1907 between Swansea Valley Jct. and Landore.

Although the Glamorgan Spelter company closed in 1907, and the Foxholes colliery before the Great War, the Llansamlet Spelter survived to 1973.

The box at Swansea Valley closed in February 1963.

In the 1870s, the double line approaching Landore Viaduct was flanked on the north side by four long sidings serving Coke Ovens and the Landore Siemens Works, access to which was controlled by Steel Works Sidings box, located close to the bridge under which ran the Swansea Vale Railway from Swansea St. Thomas to Brynamman East. This box was closed in 1892 when a new box was opened, also controlling a nest of four sidings on the down side. The box was re-sited in 1907 when the Down Goods Loop from Llansamlet came into use, ending just short of the viaduct.

A map of the area after the Great War shows that there had been further siding development on both sides of the line as the level of industry increased, notably the Mannesmann Tube Works and the Swansea Hematite Works (steelworks), both to the north. These companies lasted until after the Second World War, with the Swansea Hematite Works closing in 1945, Mannesman Tube Works in 1960, and Landore Steel Works in 1980.

About a mile to the west of Llansamlet station, the ex-Midland line from Brynamman, on its way to its various facilities located on the east bank of the River Tawe at St. Thomas, crossed beneath the South Wales Main Line. A junction on the main line at this point – Swansea Valley Jct. – connected with Six Pit Jct. on the Midland. In this view, a 'Hall' with a Cardiff to Swansea local, is seen running across the underbridge, pictured from the van of a freight train running on the Swansea Vale line. There were originally two sets of connections between the two companies' lines here: the main one to Six Pit Jct. beyond the bridge, which at one time contained a transfer shed, and another in the foreground.

NORMAN SIMMONS, CTY HUGH DAVIES

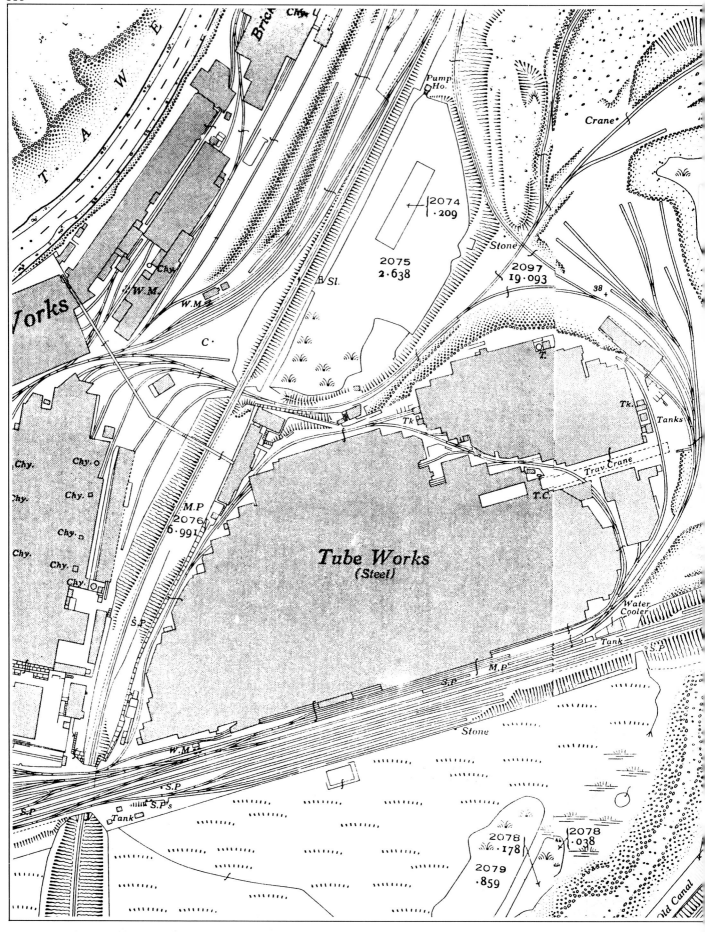

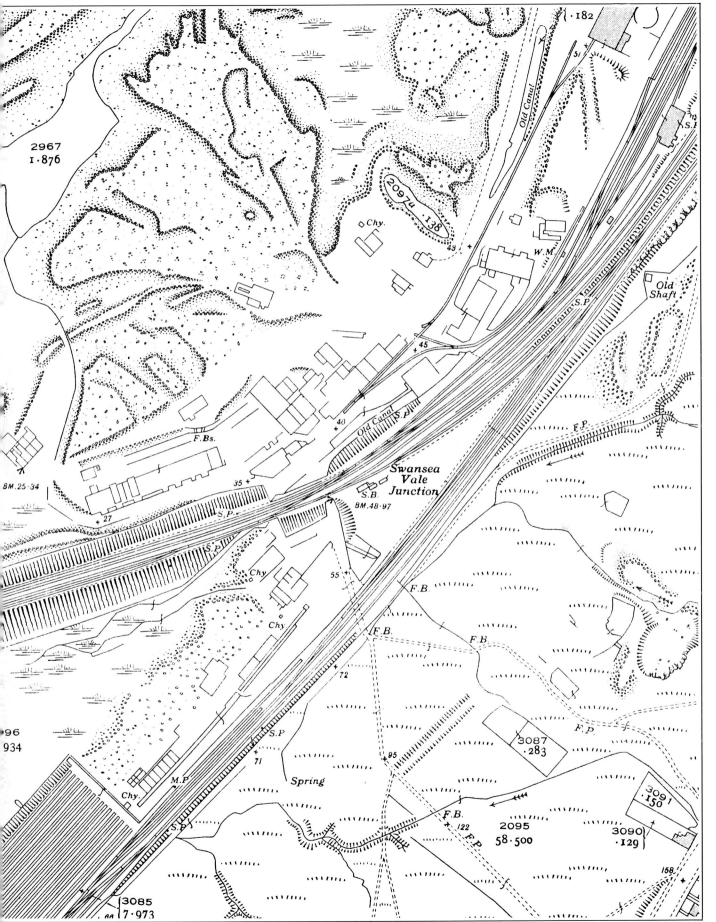

Taken from 25-inch Ordnance Survey. (Crown copyright reserved)

LANDORE VIADUCT

On the eastern approach to Landore, Brunel was faced with the prospect of crossing the valley of the River Tawe before turning south to gain access to Swansea, situated on the far bank. In addition to the river, the valley contained the Swansea Canal, and a significant area of flood plain and marshland. Brunel's solution to this was a viaduct of 599 yards length, containing 37 spans ranging from 40 to 100 feet, crossing the river at around the mid-point. The viaduct was constructed of timber.

By the 1880s the viaduct was proving to be inadequate for the increasing weight of traffic, and was in need of substantial repairs, so in 1886 a start was made on its replacement. In this, almost the entire eastern half of the viaduct was removed and an embankment substituted, its western end up against the river. The new viaduct connecting to this embankment was constructed of ironwork, carried on masonry supports, with 22 spans giving a total length of 389 yards. It now started on the eastern bank of the Tawe, and crossed to the eastern end of Landore station, by this time additionally spanning the GWR's Morriston branch.

As with all such structures, Landore viaduct was subject to routine maintenance and replacement work from time to time. Some rebuilding was carried out in 1915, whilst the decking was replaced in 1927/8. Major rebuilding took place in 1978.

Landore Viaduct, photographed in 1971, looking east, with the span over the River Tawe at the far end. The railway on the embankment beyond the viaduct was originally carried by the eastern half of the original timber viaduct, which was swept away in the 1887 rebuilding. Crossing below we can see the abandoned branch to Morriston, with Landore (Low Level) station in the right foreground. The old branch joined the main-line loop towards Swansea High St. at Hafod Jct., a half-mile further on to the right.
NATIONAL RAILWAY MUSEUM

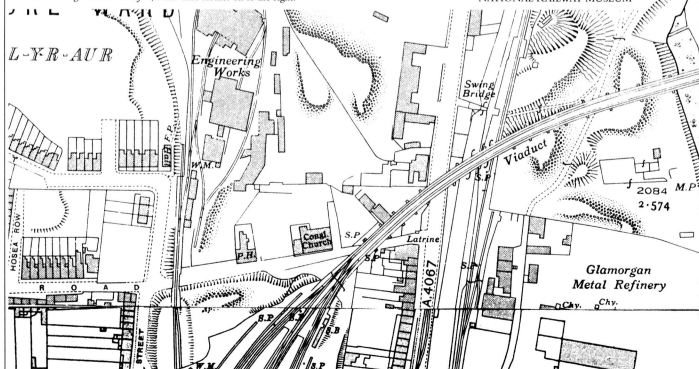

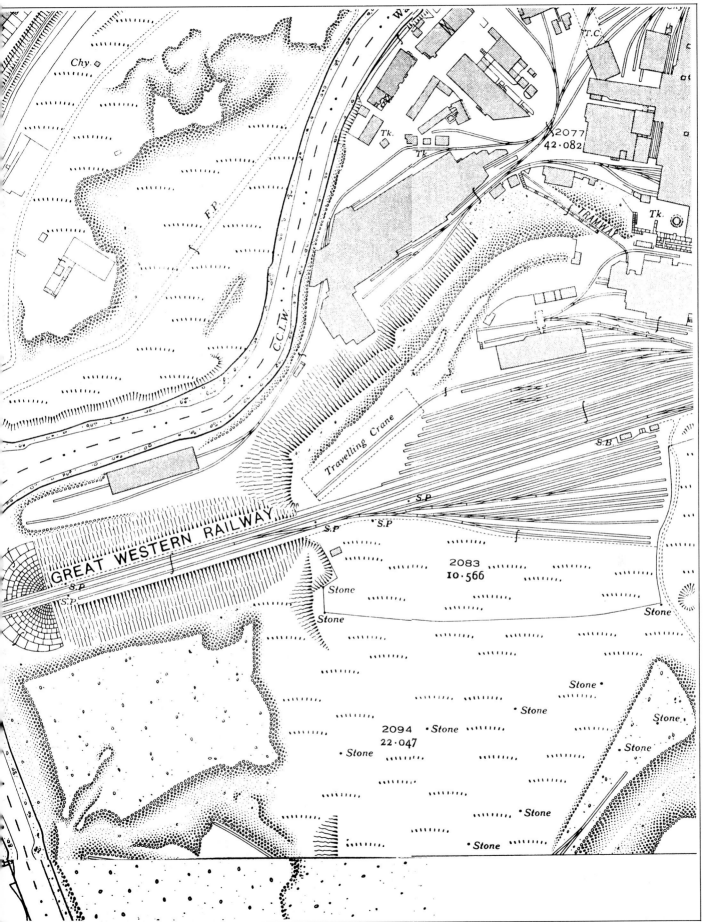

Chy.

FP.

C.C.L.W.

Travelling Crane

TRAMWAY

Tk.

Tk.

Tk.

2077
42·082

T.C.

S.B.

S.P.

S.P.

S.P.

S.P.

S.P.

S.P.

GREAT WESTERN RAILWAY.

2083
10·566

Stone

Stone

2094
22·047

Stone

Stone

Stone

Stone

Stone

Stone

Stone

Stone

Stone

Stone

Stone

Stone

Taken from 25-inch Ordnance Survey. (Crown copyright reserved)

Landore station in the 1950s, seen from the eastern edge of Landore Loco. The running lines in the foreground were those to High Street, about a mile away. Up to the 1920s, Landore was effectively the main-line station for Swansea, connected by a shuttle service over the branch to High Street, and was provided with all appropriate facilities; the station's size reflects that role. The goods shed is seen to the right of the station, though unlike the passenger facilities, this was provided entirely for local needs.

L & GRP

LANDORE STATION

Landore station in the 1870s was a relatively simple junction, with the Up and Down main lines crossing the viaduct doubled in each direction through the station to serve two island platforms. Nos. 1 and 2 signal boxes, at the east and west ends of the station respectively, controlled access. There was a small number of sidings on both routes to the west of the station, and a short line from the south side of the station had been opened to Millbrook Iron Works around this time, eventually running beneath the viaduct.

In May 1881, Landore Low Level station was opened on a line from Hafod Junction (on the branch into High Street) to Morriston, extended in May 1914 to Felin Fran West, on the recently-opened Swansea District Line. This single-platform station was situated a little to the south-east of the main-line site, close to the base of the viaduct.

In the 1880s, a connection on the north side of the station led to the Millbrook Iron Works, Vivians Works and Pentre Colliery, while on the south side, a line ran from the station sidings down under the west end of the viaduct into the Millbrook Tin Works and Landore Tinplate Co. There was also a small number of sidings on both routes to the west of the station, alongside the engine shed in the triangle between the two routes.

In 1913 a new goods shed and associated sidings were provided in an extended south yard, by which time the line into Millbrook Works had disappeared. The connections on the north side of the station into Pentre Colliery and Millbrook Engineering were still in use, the latter lasting until all the north side connections were removed in 1967.

Earliest available maps show two signal boxes at Landore: No. 1 box was located on the south side between the end of the viaduct and the platforms, and controlled the connections at the east end of the station, whilst No. 2 box, at the west end of the up platform,

controlled the junction into High Street and the Cockett direction, and also other connections, e.g. to and from the engine shed. By 1914, these boxes had been renamed Landore East and West respectively. The East box closed in April 1936, a ground frame being provided on the north side of the line to operate connections in the up yard. The West box took over control of the east end of the station, and was renamed Landore.

Whilst through trains or coaches between Swansea and London (etc.) had used High Street station from the outset, those through services bound for or running from West Wales called at Landore as the Swansea stop, with the branch trains or any through coaches providing the link. Following the lengthening of platforms at High Street station, from 1926 all through passenger trains to and from the west destined to serve Swansea were diverted to run into High Street, utilising the 1906-built west curve to and from Llanelly and West Wales. However, some Fishguard boat services with no call to make took the Swansea District route via Felin Fran. With this alteration, Landore station lost its role as a main-line junction, and in 1927, its refreshment facilities too; after this, it was served only by stopping services.

Landore Station was closed in November 1964.

The up sidings were taken out of use in 1967, together with the ground frame. Landore box remained in operation until 1st October 1973, when MAS was introduced throughout the area and a new layout brought into operation at Landore with a new crossover provided between the end of the viaduct and the newly-created Landore Junction, to be used by trains proceeding in the Cockett direction, creating single-line operation over the up line as far as the start of the Cockett line, reflecting the reduction in traffic over that route.

Landore station, looking west from the up island platform, showing the line running ahead to Swansea Loop West box, Cockett, Llanelly and the west, whilst the tight curve around to the left was the deviation into Swansea High Street. The stone buildings on the two platforms were probably original, and were a distinctive characteristic of Landore station. By this time, a single-arm signal with direction indicator served the Down Main, in this instance reading 'Down Branch', indicating a train to Swansea High Street.

LENS OF SUTTON

The view from the west end of Landore station, outside Landore box, showing the line curving left towards Swansea High Street, with Landore depot in the centre, and the line to Cockett and the west on the right. The picture shows clearly how the engine shed was located in the angle formed by the two main lines. From the left can be seen the coal stage, with roads on both sides; the lifting shop; in the distance, the 1932-built, four-road shed; and on the right of the site, the original four-road shed, dating from 1874. Access to the turntable from the main yard was given between the coal stage and lifting shop. To the right of the old shed, the Down and Up mains to Loop West box and Llanelly were separated by a siding, on which can be seen some wagons and two guard's brake vans. The line recommenced its climb to the summit at Cockett at this point, with a 1 in 52 gradient for 1½ miles to the tunnel, then easing to 1 in 70 for the final half-mile. The up sidings are seen on the extreme right-hand edge. This picture was taken on 14th June 1961 when the steam shed had just been cleared for conversion to a diesel depot.

NATIONAL RAILWAY MUSEUM

Landore box, as seen on 20th June 1968, still with another five years use ahead of it before overtaken by MAS in the area. The box was located at the west end of the up platform, originally the site of the old No. 2 box. This box, as Landore West, was extended to take over control of the full station layout in 1936 when the East box was closed, and renamed Landore from that time. All train movements over Landore viaduct, through the station and over the curve onto the branch to the west of the station, and vice versa, were limited by speed restrictions of either 10 or 20 mph. Here, a 15 mph restriction was in force for eastbound movements at this point.

R. H. MARROWS

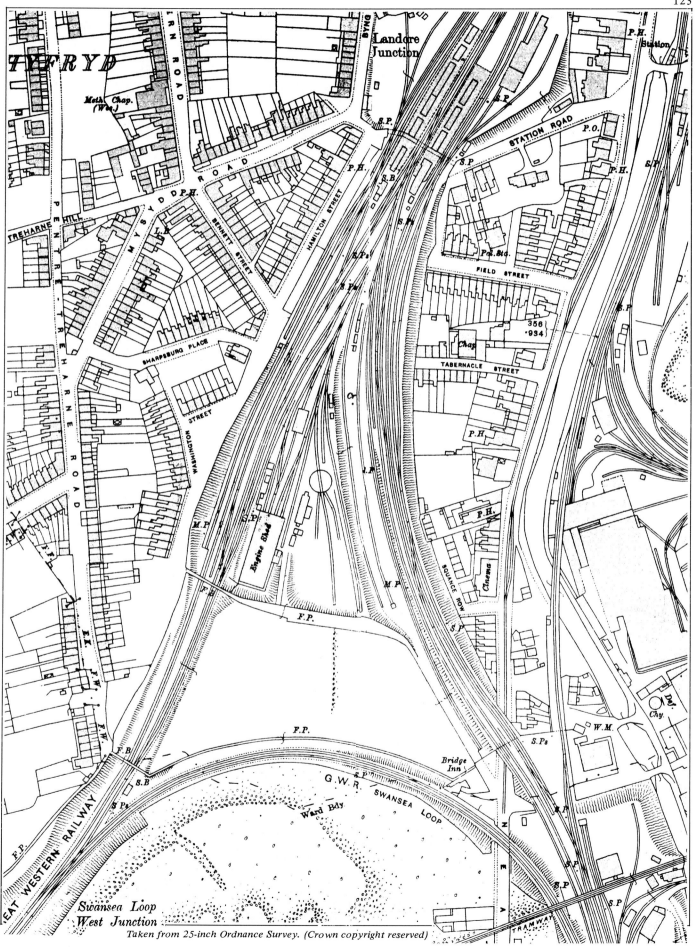

Taken from 25-inch Ordnance Survey. (Crown copyright reserved)

Landore depot as it will be best remembered to those who knew it, with up to 21 'Castles' allocated in 1960/61. Here, we see no fewer than eight in this picture, probably taken in 1959, the two in the foreground being Nos. 5041 *Tiverton Castle* and 5004 *Llanstephan Castle*, with a lone '41 XX' (possibly No. 4107) on the far side. The picture probably records the early afternoon line-up, when several 'Castles' were being prepared for workings to London on the 2.30, 3.45, 4.35 and 5.30 p.m. services, with others going west to Carmarthen, and perhaps a Swindon engine among them to work the 3.50 p.m. Whitland to Kensington Milk from Felin Fran. HUW DANIEL

LANDORE MPD

Locomotive facilities were provided at Swansea from the outset, with a shed a little way to the north of High Street station, on the west side of the running lines. This two-road shed, with turntable and the usual coal, water and servicing facilities, was closed in 1874, and the new goods shed constructed on its site, incorporating a little of the old engine shed within its structure.

Facilities were then opened at Landore, located to the west of the station within the angle of the two diverging routes. These comprised a four-road shed, stop-blocked at its western end, situated alongside the lines to Carmarthen, with a coal stage to its east. A turntable (45ft, in 1905) and three sidings were provided to the south, alongside the High Street line.

At the beginning of 1902, Landore had an allocation of 30 engines, made up of:

3	'806/2201' 2-4-0s (Nos. 822, 2207, 2219)	
1	'56' 2-4-0 (No. 719)	
1	'Stella' 2-4-0 (No. 3202)	
1	'3521' 4-4-0 (No. 3556)	
6	0-6-0s (including 1 '2301')	
1	'Metro' 2-4-0T	
20	0-6-0PT and 0-6-0ST	

The 2-4-0s worked the London expresses starting from Swansea, though they would soon be replaced by 'Dukes', whilst the 0-6-0s were utilised on the lesser passenger duties, and goods services. The 0-6-0 tank engines, many of which were, of course, saddle tanks, would have been used on local yard shunting and tripping but also on banking trains up Cockett bank, viz. the ill-fated saddle tank in the Loughor accident of 1904.

To the west of Swansea at this time were five '2201' class 2-4-0s based at Carmarthen Junction, while New Milford had two 'Atbara' 4-4-0s, two '2201' 2-4-0s, a 'Barnum' 2-4-0, two '3521' 4-4-0s and one of the 7ft. 'Sir Daniel 2-2-2s. Each depot also had a selection of 0-6-0s, 0-6-0PT and STs. In 1902, the larger passenger engines would have been working regularly through Landore en route east. Following the opening of the Swansea Loop line in 1906, passenger engines from sheds to the west would also have worked daily into High Street, and been a common sight at Landore shed.

Landore received some '28XX' engines in the 1900s, and by 1910, three were allocated. Their exact duties are not known, but they were used for banking turns between Landore or Gowerton and Cockett.

Until the rebuilding of High Street station in the mid-1920s, when platforms were lengthened to take full-length Paddington services, the Landore allocation of 4-4-0 main-line passenger engines remained between seven and ten, but in the early 1920s rose to between ten and twelve. 'Bulldogs' appeared to be the most popular and in 1906 accounted for nine of the ten 4-4-0s allocated. Two 'Dukes' were allocated from late 1902, with 'Atbaras' between 1907 and 1927, 'Badmintons' from 1911 to 1927, and 'Flowers' from 1909 to 1928. A 'City' class 4-4-0 was allocated spasmodically between 1908 and 1914, and the County 4-4-0 had a single presence in 1906/7, 1915 and 1922-26, with two allocated during 1922–23.

With the service replanning in 1926, the Landore allocation changed dramatically. In 1923/4, three 'Saints' had been progressively allocated, but in 1926 the allocation became ten by year end, with thirteen in 1927 and fifteen in 1928, before reducing again to

The east end of Landore 'new' shed around 1961, with single-chimney 'Castle' 5091 *Cleeve Abbey* (of Landore) and double-chimney 5032 *Usk Castle* (Old Oak) standing 'head up' (for London), with a '56XX' on the furthest road. The lifting/repair shop is seen on the left, a familiar Great Western design, with the turntable beyond it, whilst the coal stage was just off the left-hand edge of the picture.

Along with Canton and Old Oak, Landore shed supplied motive power for London trains to the east of Swansea, utilising 'Castles' for the turns from the early 1930s. By 1939, the shed had eleven of the class to work seven turns, and in 1959, twenty engines were for fourteen turns, when six Landore engines were to be seen daily at Paddington, whilst others ran to the west as far as Fishguard. Here, No. 4099 *Kilgerran Castle* is seen at her home shed, Landore, on 11th August 1959. A West Country engine from 1936, No. 4099 was transferred to Swansea in November 1957.

N. E. PREEDY

around a dozen, then eight by the end of 1931. All had been transferred out in favour of 'Stars' by the end of 1932.

Auto engines of the '517' class appeared at Landore around 1922 for services over the Morriston branch to Felin Fran or Llandarcy Platform, with one morning service almost completing a circle by working into Swansea East Dock. Formerly, services over the branch to Felin Fran had been operated by the local 'shuttle' sets connecting Swansea and Landore.

Following the introduction of 'Castles' and 'Kings' on the West of England services, 'Stars' were first tried at Landore in 1928/9 when 4062 *Malmesbury Abbey* was allocated from July 1928 to May 1929 and 4057 *Princess Elizabeth* from August to October 1928. Following an absence of two years, they reappeared during the second half of 1931 by which time the 'Saint' allocation was in decline. There were nine 'Stars' at Landore by the end of 1931, and thirteen by the end of 1932, heralding a long association with the depot, until they in turn were deposed by 'Castles'. During 1938, the number of 'Stars' allocated fell to six, remained at five all through the war years, and then, as the class was withdrawn from service, lasted out in single numbers until January 1953, when 4048

Landore 'Castle' No. 5039 *Rhuddlan Castle* seen at the depot on 11th October 1959. New in June 1935, No. 5039 was allocated first to Old Oak Common, where she remained until June 1952 with a very high reputation among the 'Castle' fleet there, often working the 'Cheltenham Flyer' until 1939. Between December 1946 and September 1948, she ran as an oil-burner in an experiment to test the practicality of using oil against coal, good quality steam coal being in short supply after the war. She moved to Carmarthen in June 1952, then to Landore in June 1957, returning to Carmarthen in September 1960. Following moves to several depots during 1963/4 as steam traction drew to an end on the Western, her final working depot was Reading (until June 1964), where she was kept for replacement of failed diesels on through expresses. No. 5039 returned to Swansea after withdrawal, being sold as scrap to George Cohen & Sons at Morriston in June 1964, having totalled a mileage of 1.381 million.

Landore 'Castle' No. 5077 *Fairey Battle* is seen on the coal stage road on 11th October 1959. Built as *Eastnor Castle* in 1938, she was renamed *Fairey Battle* in late 1940 as part of a series featuring aircraft in use with the RAF and RN (FAA) at that time. No. 5077 was initially allocated to Old Oak Common, but in March 1939 was transferred to Taunton, and to Cardiff Canton in September 1950. She moved to Bath Road in 1954, and to Landore in July 1956, remaining there until the depot closed in September 1961, when she was moved to Llanelly. Withdrawn in July 1962 with a mileage of 1.089m, she was sold as scrap to R.S. Hayes of Bridgend.

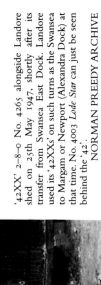

A view of the 1932 shed at Landore on 9th July 1950, with the repair shop and boiler room to the left of the four-road main building. This view shows Landore's pannier No. 9738 and 'Castle' No. 7018 *Drysllwyn Castle*, with Old Oak 'County' No. 1000 *County of Middlesex* (with original-style double chimney) to the right. No. 5051 *Earl Bathurst* can be seen at the side of the shed, on the extreme right. No. 1000 was mostly to be seen on Bristol and West Country trains out of Paddington at this time, but occasionally she travelled into South Wales, and was recorded on Carmarthen and Fishguard trains around this time. She was transferred to Laira in December 1950, and to Chester in October 1952, but moved to Bath Road in March 1954; from this time, No. 1000 was often seen on the 5.50 a.m. Bristol and 7.35 a.m. Cardiff trains to Swansea, returning east with the 10.50 a.m. Swansea (8.20 a.m. Neyland to Paddington) as far as Cardiff.

G. DOUGLAS, CTY. R. K. BLENCOWE

'42XX' 2–8–0 No. 4265 alongside Landore shed on 25th May 1947, shortly after its transfer from Swansea East Dock. Landore used its '42XXs' on such turns as the Swansea to Margam or Newport (Alexandra Dock) at that time. No. 4003 *Lode Star* can just be seen behind the '42'.

NORMAN PREEDY ARCHIVE

Princess Victoria was withdrawn. The other four 'Stars' at Landore from 1950 were:

4003 *Lode Star* (w/drawn Jul 51 and preserved)
4023 (unnamed from 1939 – w/drawn Jul 50)
4039 *Queen Matilda* (w/drawn Nov 50)
4050 *Princess Alice* (w/drawn Feb 52)

Landore 'Stars', in company with those at Carmarthen, where two or three were based from 1924–27, with one during 1928/9, worked the West Wales to Paddington services with distinction between the 'Saint' and 'Castle' eras.

A second four-road shed was added at Landore in 1932, to the south-west of the original structure, with improved repair facilities attached. The turntable, now a 65ft unit, was re-sited southwest-wards alongside it to facilitate the addition and lengthening of various other depot sidings. A new coal stage was located to the south-east of the new shed.

The first 'Castle' to be allocated to Landore was 5009 *Shrewsbury Castle* in July 1932, followed by 4074 *Caldicot Castle* (which was to have a long association with the depot) in July 1933. By the end of 1934, there were six 'Castles' allocated, largely replacing the 'Stars' on the London services.

Landore-based 'Star' No. 4023 seen at the front end of the later covered shed on 9th September 1951. First allocated to Landore in January 1932, she was transferred to Bath Road in June 1933, but returned in December 1935 for a stay that lasted until she was withdrawn in July 1952, except for a short spell at Worcester during mid-1942. Built in 1909, she retained inside steam pipes throughout, and her final mileage was 1,912,170. No.4023 was originally named *King George*, but this was removed with the introduction of the 'King' Class in 1927, when she became *Danish Monarch*, though these plates were removed in 1939 with the outbreak of war.   H. C. CASSERLEY

A visitor from Old Oak: No. 5087 *Tintern Abbey* is seen in 1961, ready for departure off shed. Around this time, Old Oak engines worked the 1.30 and 2.30 p.m. (12.5 p.m. Milford Haven) from Swansea High Street back to Paddington, as well as the 9.35 p.m. overnight service.

Landore-based 'Castle' No. 7021 *Haverfordwest Castle* standing at the east end of the yard on 10th May 1953, showing clear signs of favourable care and attention, which augured well for the future at the depot. The engine went new to Landore in June 1949, and with the exception of odd spells at Carmarthen, remained at Landore virtually all her working life, other than after Landore closed for dieselisation, when she went to Llanelly. It was common practice to move high-mileage 'Castles' from Landore to Carmarthen so that they could finish their time coming up to main works overhaul working on class 'C' services from that depot. When ex-works, they then returned to Landore, though Carmarthen did retain No. 7021 when released after a Heavy Intermediate at Swindon in January 1958 for nearly 17 months.   R.K. BLENCOWE

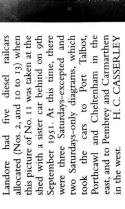

Landore had five diesel railcars allocated (Nos. 2, and 10 to 13) when this picture of No. 11 was taken at the shed with a sister car behind on 9th September 1951. At this time, there were three Saturdays-excepted and two Saturdays-only diagrams, which took the cars to Port Talbot, Porthcawl and Cheltenham in the east, and to Pembrey and Carmarthen in the west.   H.C. CASSERLEY

In 1937, Landore received a diesel railcar for a diagram of main-line stopping services from Swansea to Llanelly, Port Talbot, Whitland, and Kidwelly. In the postwar era, Swansea's cars also served Porthcawl, and made a lengthy run to Cheltenham.

The number of 'Castles' at Landore gradually increased with between ten and twelve through the war years, thirteen and fifteen between 1946–49, sixteen and nineteen between 1950 and 1959, finally rising to twenty-one during the halcyon days of 1960/1, when the Landore allocation was in its prime. The high allocation reflected the fact that all the Landore turns to London were overnight, and involved two engines in the diagram. Landore became synonymous with 'Castles' in pristine condition, and they were a sight to behold from about 1957–61 in charge of the 'Pembroke Coast Express' and 'South Wales Pullman', in gleaming condition with silver painted buffers (though apparently this was basically to make for easier recognition at Old Oak Common!).

A snapshot of the Landore allocation at the end of 1953 showed:

17	'Castle' 4-6-0s
8	'Hall' 4-6-0s
2	'41XX' 2-6-2Ts
5	'72XX' 2-8-2Ts
8	'56XX' 0-6-2Ts
3	'64XX' 0-6-0PTs
1	'16XX' 0-6-0PTs
12	'57XX' 0-6-0PTs and 1 Diesel Railcar.

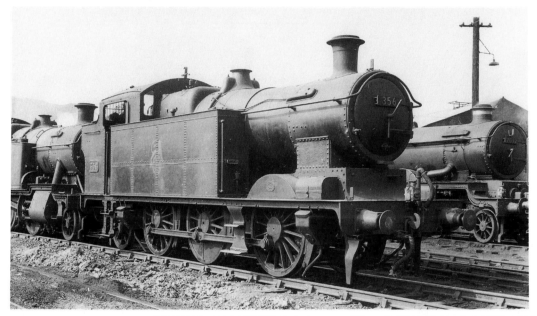

Ex-Taff Vale 'Class As' were not a common sight at Landore shed, even though they operated into High Street on the Treherbert services – they tended to work straight back with the return journey. Abercynon's No. 356 would have been a rare visitor indeed, and is seen here at the depot on 10th May 1953, along with two more common types – Landore 'Castle' No. 7012 *Barry Castle* and a '72XX'. It would be interesting to learn how the Abercynon engine had contrived to reach this shed.
T. J. EDGINGTON

Newport (Ebbw Jct) '42XX' No. 5256 at Landore shed on 4th May 1952. At this time, there were through freights from Rogerstone to Landore Steelworks scheduled for '42' haulage, which may have been the duty worked by this engine. RAY HINTON

Another view of the front end of the 1932 shed on 9th September 1951, with Landore 'Hall' No. 6918 *Sandon Hall* at the head of a line of engines on the road that ran alongside the western side of the building. The general poor state of cleanliness of all the engines on view was characteristic of the position on the Western Region at this time, with few depots – Cardiff Canton being a significant exception – paying much attention to presentation. The scene is not enhanced by the rather drab backdrop provided by the high ground beyond.
H. C. CASSERLEY

The final Landore 'Star' was No. 4048 *Princess Victoria*, seen here standing alongside the 1932 shed on 9th September 1951. First allocated to Landore in September 1932, she moved to Worcester in 1934/5, but returned to Landore in June 1935 and remained there until withdrawal in January 1953, by which time she had run 1,770,921 miles. She was one of the 'Stars' fitted with 'Castle'-type outside steam pipes. During the war and postwar era, No.4048 was occasionally recorded at Paddington with Welsh expresses, though her more regular duties involved workings to Cardiff and Carmarthen, sometimes both in one diagram. A Landore 'Star' had the distinction of working the first of the postwar 'Ports-to-Ports' services to and from Newcastle from Swansea to Banbury and back.
R. M. CASSERLEY

'64XXs' were used on auto services to Carmarthen, and the '72s' *inter alia* on banking up to Cockett.

The shed's allocation in 1959 included twenty 'Castles' (for 14 turns), eight 'Halls' (5 turns), two '22XXs' (1 turn), three '28XXs' (2 turns), six '56XXs' (5 turns), two '51XXs' (1 turn), and five '72XXs' (4 turns), with sixteen 0-6-0Ts for local and shunting duties.

In June 1961 Landore closed for conversion to a diesel depot and the 'Castles' for working east of Swansea were largely transferred to Neath, while those for working west went to Llanelly. One Llanelly engine, however, worked to London to preserve route knowledge for the Landore men now working from Llanelly. Neath depot was therefore largely charged with upholding the enviable Landore reputation for presentation in the final years of steam operation on the main line. Those engines used on local shunting, tripping, and freight working went to Swansea East Dock.

Also on shed at Landore on 9th September 1951 was the original 'Hall', No. 4900 *Saint Martin*, seen here standing in front of *Princess Victoria*. During September 1951, this engine was transferred from Wolverhampton (Stafford Road) to Banbury, and was probably a Banbury engine here; Stafford Road locomotives were rare in South Wales, especially as far west as Swansea, but Banbury engines had daily freight workings on iron ore and other traffic for the steelworks. *Saint Martin* was, of course, of the 'Saint' class – No. 2925 – and was the engine selected in 1924 to receive smaller driving wheels (reduced from 6ft 8½ ins to 6ft), and a 'Castle' type cab, making her the first of what became the 'Hall' class. In a career stretching from September 1907 to April 1959, she amassed a total of 2,092,500 miles, making her one of only four ex-GWR engines to top the 2 million-mile mark.   R. M. CASSERLEY

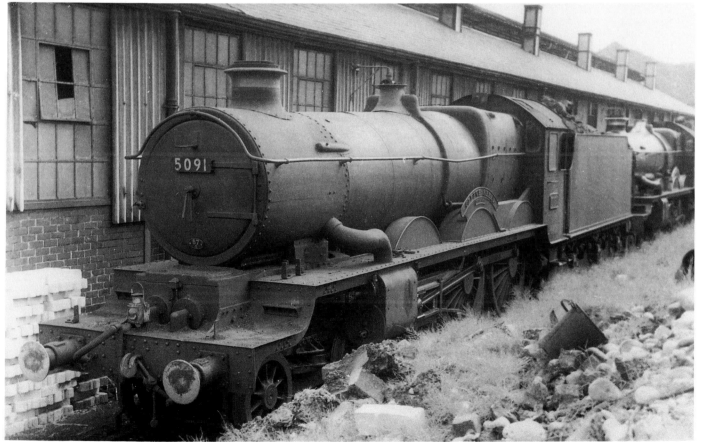

'Castle' No. 5091 *Cleeve Abbey*, here seen alongside the shed on 25th August 1959, became a Landore engine in July 1958, having moved from Carmarthen after heavy overhaul at Swindon. She continued to work from Swansea until Landore closed, when she went to Llanelly, but then moved on to Cardiff Canton/East Dock until April 1964. This engine was a rebuild of 'Star' No. 4071, and re-appeared in her new guise after three months at Swindon factory, in December 1938.

F. A. BLENCOWE, CTY. R. K. BLENCOWE

Rounding the tight curve from Landore station, within the final mile home, Landore 'Castle' No. 5016 *Montgomery Castle* was heading the down 'South Wales Pullman', 8.50 a.m. ex-Paddington, towards Hafod Jct. in the summer of 1959. For the engine, this was the return working of the previous day's up 'Pembroke Coast Express' (3.45 p.m. Swansea). In order to travel by the Pullman train at this time, passengers on the 8.50 a.m. for Swansea would have to pay an additional 10 shillings for First class, and 5 shillings for Second class, on top of the 47s 9d First single or 31s 10d Second single fares. The engine still had a single chimney, which it would retain until early 1961.

HUW DANIEL

Into the varying gradients on the mile-long climb through Loop East and Hafod Jct. to Landore, Old Oak Common 'Castle' No. 5043 Earl of Mount Edgcumbe, was blasting its way along the Up Main with what was probably a Saturday relief service to Paddington, while a Canton 'Britannia' was standing at Landore with the 9.12 a.m. Cardiff to Neyland parcels. The latter was scheduled to call at Landore, then take the direct line to Cockett and the west, and on this occasion was standing on the loop sidings on the inside of the curve from Landore.

HUW DANIEL

HAFOD & LOOP EAST JUNCTIONS

Hafod Junction, with the line leading to Landore LL and Morriston on the extreme right of this view. Landore 'Castle' No. 7012 *Barry Castle* is seen heading down the short 1 in 37 incline towards Loop East Jct. and High Street station with the down South Wales Pullman in May 1959. The first three cars were Second class, followed by a Bar Kitchen car, three First class Kitchen or Parlour cars, and another Brake Second bringing up the rear. HUW DANIEL

When the South Wales main line was opened in 1850, it had an uninterrupted run into Swansea from Landore. This changed in May 1881 with the opening of the line to Morriston, the junction for which was at Hafod, a short distance to the south of Landore engine shed, and almost a mile from High Street. A double junction was established at this point, although the branch soon became single line. With the completion of the Swansea District line in 1913, the branch was extended from Morriston to Felin Fran, with the ability to act as a diversionary route to and from the London direction in the event of blockage of the main line between Hafod and Skewen.

During the 19th century, the pattern of trains at Landore was very largely that of through movements on each route, with only a handful of trains (goods, but also one passenger) reversing direction at Landore to run between Swansea and Llanelly or beyond. Passengers travelling between Swansea and the west were, for the most part, obliged to change at Landore.

In 1906, the Landore West Curve was opened, linking the line into and out of High Street with the Landore to Cockett line, the controlling boxes being Swansea Loop East Junction (a little over a half-mile from High Street), and West Junction (1¼ miles out of High St.), at the bottom of Cockett bank. From this time, trains could run directly from the West into High Street, and vice-versa, but only local passenger trains and goods traffic did so. This arrangement changed in 1926, as has been mentioned above, from when nearly all through passenger traffic called at High Street before reversing to continue its journey.

A large new yard was opened at 'Maliphant Street' for full-load traffic in 1906. Hafod Yard contained three pairs of sidings and a single siding with roads between for the working of wagons of coal, hay and other mileage traffic, and was located to the west of the Swansea Loop East box.

The Loop West Junction box was destroyed by enemy bombing in 1941, but was quickly restored.

Hafod Junction was removed after the closure of the Morriston Branch in September 1962, whilst the two Loop boxes were removed under the MAS scheme.

A close-up view of the start of the Morriston branch in the foreground, showing the Hafod Junction Starting signals for the up main line (located on the down side because of the track curvature) and the branch in September 1953. The branch crossed over the canal shortly beyond the junction, then ran alongside it to pass beneath Landore Viaduct. P. J. GARLAND

Old Oak Common 'Castle' No. 7020 *Gloucester Castle* heading the 11.5 a.m. Milford Haven to Paddington (1.30 p.m. ex-Swansea) past Hafod on Thursday, 30th April 1959. This was the return working of the 6.55 p.m. Paddington to Fishguard train (OOC Turn 26), that the 'Castle' was scheduled to bring into Swansea at 11.11 p.m. the previous night. The '071' reporting number for this train was in use only from September 1958 to June 1959, becoming '073' for the following summer service. During the period from Winter 58/9 to Winter 59/60, all services to London carried '0XX' or '1XX' numbers, a system which was to give way to the 3-character 'AXX' for steam power in Summer 1960. Diesels carried a 'T' prefix to indicate the class, whilst the steam engines retained 'A' headlamps to signify this.   HUW DANIEL

The 12.5 p.m. (summer Saturdays only) Pembroke Dock to Paddington (2.50 p.m. ex-Swansea) climbing out of Hafod Jct. behind Reading 'Castle' No. 5076 *Gladiator* on Saturday, 15th July 1961. On weekdays, the Pembroke coaches were attached to the earlier 12.5 p.m. Milford at Whitland, but on Saturdays the traffic warranted separate trains. The front portion of the train (at least) contained ex-LNER stock, which was probably working back to its home region via London. Swansea regularly saw such coaches on the York & Newcastle services, and they appear to have been substituting as the Swansea portion of the London express on this occasion. The line between Swansea Loop East & West is on the embankment to the right.
                                        R. O. TUCK

The 12.5 p.m. Milford Haven to Paddington (2.30 p.m. ex-Swansea) running around the curve from Hafod Jct. towards Landore shed and station behind Landore 'Castle' No. 5041 *Tiverton Castle* on Saturday, 15th July 1961. Though only 4 months out of Swindon since her last Heavy Intermediate repair, she had lost her Landore sheen, though had been treated to painted buffers. Modifications to the shed to accommodate diesel power were by this time in hand, with the new access to the southern end of the shed being provided by the pointwork in the left foreground. The buffer stop had been removed from a siding, and left isolated alongside the main lines.

R. O. TUCK

Gloucester 'Modified Hall' No. 6985 *Parwick Hall* with the 4.20 p.m. Swansea to Paddington on Sunday, 6th July 1958. Gloucester engines were seen daily at Cardiff, but were not so familiar at Swansea. The 'Swansea Loop' line can be seen at a higher level on the extreme right, climbing at 1 in 60 to join the main/avoiding line at Loop West Jct. and an even steeper gradient up to the summit at Cockett. The London-bound line on which the train was running also climbed, but at easier gradients overall than that on the Swansea Loop.

R. O. TUCK

138

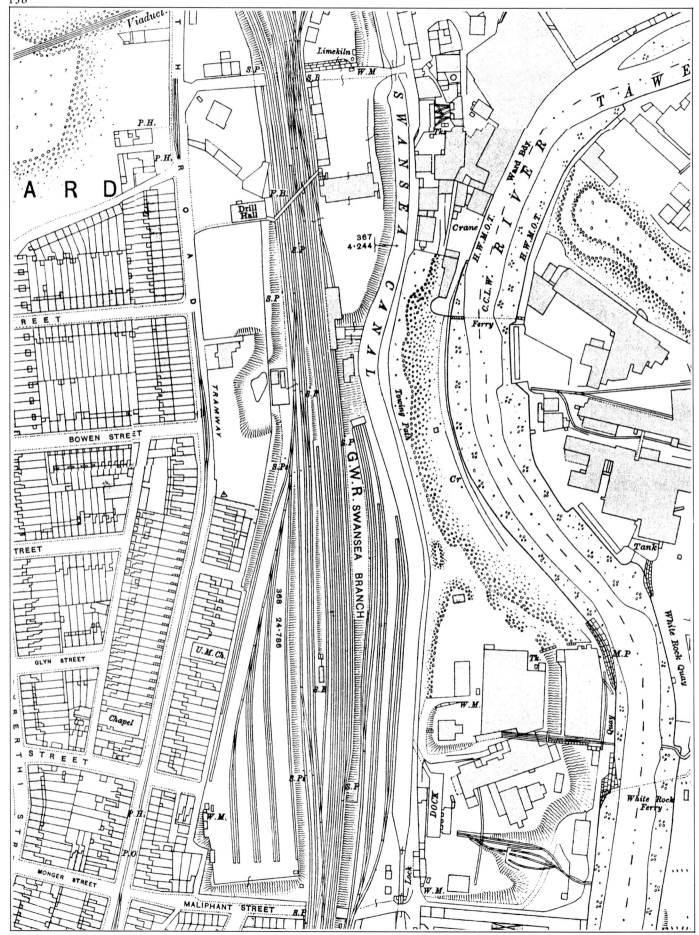

Taken from 25-inch Ordnance Survey. (Crown copyright reserved)

Hafod Junction in September 1953, showing the signal box in the extreme right foreground, with the Morriston branch lines coming off the main lines and feeding off to the right just beyond it. The main lines are seen in the centre, curving to the left, with, on the extreme left, the loop lines linking High Street with the Landore to Cockett line, opened in 1906, and controlled by Swansea Loop East and Loop West boxes at either end. Around the corner, the main line would swing hard over to the right and continue its climb to Landore station. When Sunday engineering work was in progress in the Landore area of the main line, services to the east used the Morriston branch as a diversionary route out onto the District line to Felin Fran, rejoining the main line at Skewen. P. J. GARLAND

EAST LOOP JUNCTION

Only after some 50 years of operations into Swansea was a direct line built to link High Street station with West Wales, and this opened in March 1906 for goods, and in the following May for passenger traffic. Swansea Loop East box – seen here on 21st September 1963, looking south – controlled the southern access to the link line (seen running to the right of the box), with Loop West box at the other end, on the Landore & Cockett line. This southerly junction was located to the north of the goods depot sidings, alongside New Hafod Sidings, later Hafod Yard Full Load depot (at the higher level, seen on the right). In this picture, the road was set for a down train from Landore into High Street, the two signal posts on the right-hand section of the bracket controlling exit from the Loop Line. In both cases, the lower speed signal refered to the North Dock Branch. P. J. GARLAND

The new 3-floor goods warehouse at Swansea with the goods shed beyond, seen from the main lines in May 1931, looking south towards the terminus. This structure was built in concrete and steel over an existing (and extended) goods shed platform.
WELSH INDUSTRIAL & MARITIME MUSEUM

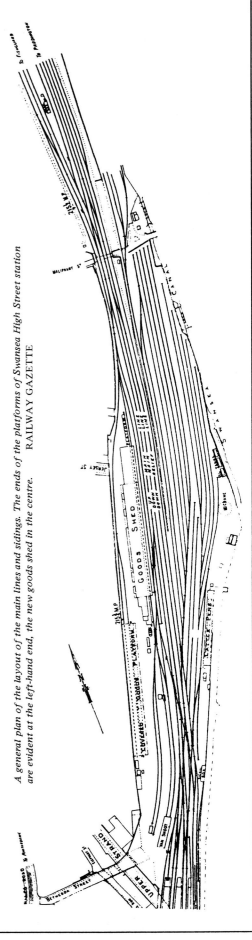

A general plan of the layout of the main lines and sidings. The ends of the platforms of Swansea High Street station are evident at the left-hand end, the new goods shed in the centre.   RAILWAY GAZETTE

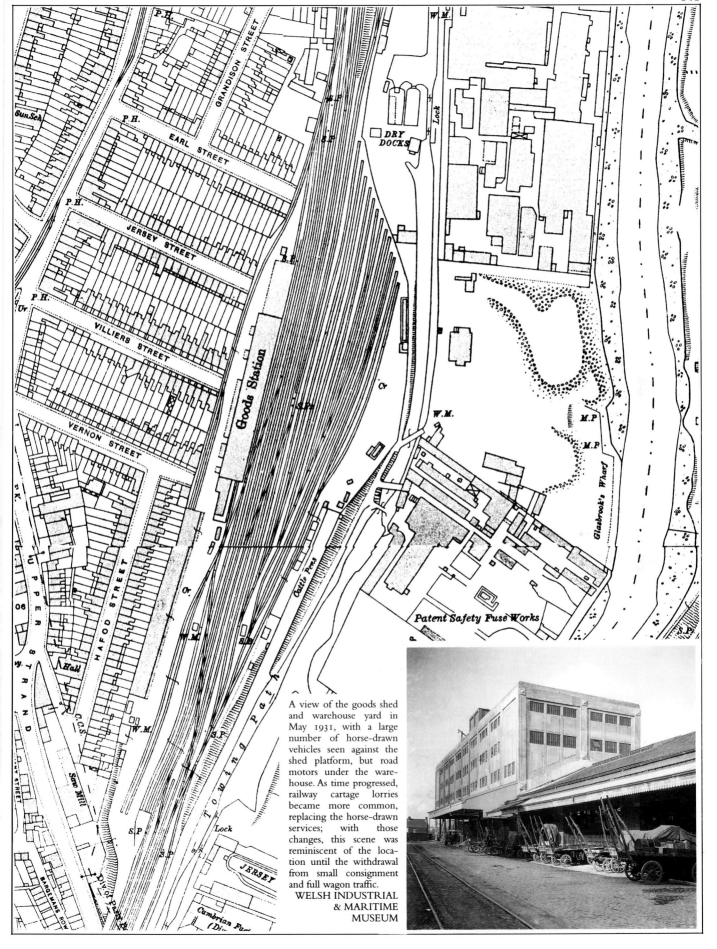

A view of the goods shed and warehouse yard in May 1931, with a large number of horse-drawn vehicles seen against the shed platform, but road motors under the warehouse. As time progressed, railway cartage lorries became more common, replacing the horse-drawn services; with those changes, this scene was reminiscent of the location until the withdrawal from small consignment and full wagon traffic.

WELSH INDUSTRIAL
& MARITIME
MUSEUM

142

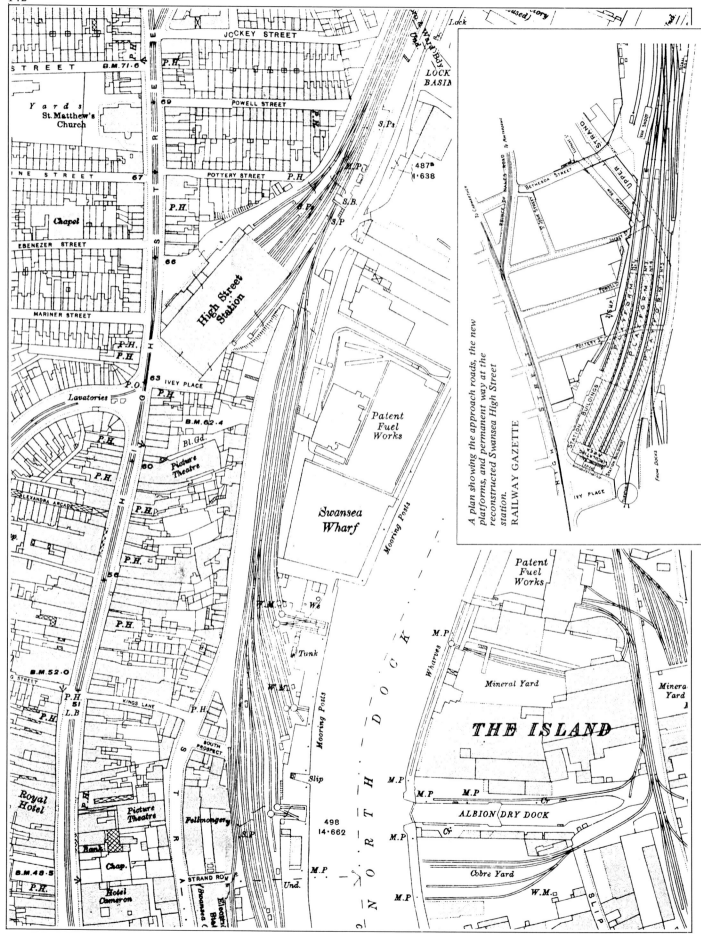

A plan showing the approach roads, the new platforms, and permanent way at the reconstructed Swansea High Street station.
RAILWAY GAZETTE

Taken from 25-inch Ordnance Survey. (Crown copyright reserved)

SWANSEA HIGH STREET

The approaches to Swansea High Street with Landore 'Prairie' tank No. 4107 arriving at Swansea with the five-coach 2.5 p.m. from Porthcawl on Saturday, 30th April 1960. This train ran via the west loop at Pyle, with its first call at Port Talbot, then all stations to High Street, due at 3.5 p.m. The '51XX' class was mostly associated with the Northern lines; in the Neath Loco Division, one example appeared at Pembroke Dock as early as 1930 for a couple of years, and two others were sent to Neath and Llanelly in 1939, both moving on to Whitland during 1940. Landore received its first – No. 4134, from Whitland – in May 1945, although No. 4107 did not arrive until October 1952.

The mile-long section of line between Landore and High Street running alongside the Swansea Canal was a hive of activity, with main-line passenger traffic approaching and leaving through Landore or over the Swansea Loop line, light engines running between Landore shed and High Street station, Morriston line traffic joining or leaving at Hafod Jct., movement of empty stock between the station and the carriage sidings, goods trips to and from Eastern Depot with inwards wagons for Swansea Goods and Hafod Yard with returning outwards loaded and empties, and the shunting of both yards. There were major installations on both sides of the line, with Maliphant Carriage Servicing and Maintenance Sidings on the down side just south of Hafod Jct., directly opposite which on the up side was Hafod (full load) Mileage Yard, with Swansea Loop East box and junction sandwiched between the yard and the main line. Between the southern end of these sidings and High Street station were two further parallel installations: on the down side, ten carriage holding and cleaning sidings, with three goods sidings on their east side, and Swansea goods shed on the up side. At the southern end of all this activity stood the High Street terminus station, some 191 miles from Paddington via Badminton.

The first station at Swansea was constructed in 1849 in Pottery Field, between High Street and the Strand. It was a wooden structure, with a single-span train shed over the ends of the two platforms; there were three roads between them, the centre of which was for stock storage. On the departure (west) side were the booking and other offices, whilst just outside, adjoining the approach, was the goods shed.

On the east side of the passenger station, a line ran to the North Dock, where early coal drops were provided for the loading of coal into moored vessels, and this took the name of the Swansea Coal Branch, opened in June 1852, lasting until 1965.

During the 1860 and 70s, there was much interest from the local population in the creation of a joint 'Central' station for Swansea, to be served by existing and intended railway companies. Their proposals were encouraged by the poor facilities then offered at High Street and Landore stations, which drew constant criticism. A Bill was put to Parliament in 1866 to that effect, but was rejected. Plans were resurrected during the early 1870s, but were finally overtaken by the GWR's proposals for their new High Street Station of 1876.

The new station on the site of the present High Street station was opened in 1876 as traffic levels grew beyond the capacity of the original station. The new station was of a basic 'open rectangle' terminus station design, with an arrival platform on the east side and a departure platform on the west (town) side, and two tracks between the platform roads for holding empty stock and vans. The platforms were 358ft long, equivalent to about eleven 6-wheel coaches then in use, or perhaps five or six bogie coaches.

By 1879, this had been extended on the departure side by making the previous single-face platform into an island, and adding a new single-face platform to its west, creating four main platform faces in total. The southern part of the station was contained within a train shed of two roof spans. The throat connections at the station were controlled from No. 6 Cabin (High St. box) located just north of the arrival platform and straddling the North Dock branch line. In 1897, a fish jetty was brought into use outside the far end of No. 1 platform, and used for both inwards and outwards traffic.

With tender piled high for the 191-mile run to Paddington, Old Oak Common men on Turn 232 were working away from Swansea on their lodging turn engine, 'Castle' No. 7027 *Thornbury Castle*, with the 11.10 a.m Milford Haven to Paddington (1.30 p.m. from Swansea) on 24th January 1959. This was the return working of the previous day's 6.55 p.m. Paddington to Fishguard Harbour, which both engine and men had worked through to Swansea. The 11.10 Milford train arriving at Swansea was programmed for a three-coach portion from Pembroke leading, and a similar rake from Milford behind. A six-coach section, including a dining car, was added to the rear with the departure engine. A selection of vans on the goods shed siding behind the departing train indicates a still-thriving small consignment ('sundries') traffic.

HUW DANIEL

'Castle' No. 5054 *Earl of Ducie*, then based at Old Oak Common, bringing the 11.55 a.m. from Paddington through the scissors crossover into platform 4 at Swansea High Street on 30th April 1960. Here, the four-coach restaurant car section at the rear would have been detached, and the train would have gone forward formed with the portions to Pembroke Dock and Milford Haven. Around seven restaurant car workings in each direction were added to and detached from West Wales trains calling at High Street daily. Landore's No. 5913 *Rushton Hall* is also seen off the end of platform 5, on the dock line.

On the east side, the arrival platform was later extended to 583ft, with a capacity of an engine and around eight bogie coaches.

The new Swansea goods shed built around this time was situated a little way out from the passenger station on the western side of the running lines, on the site of the original South Wales Railway engine shed; indeed, part of that old structure was built into the new goods shed, which was 360ft long and some 40ft wide, with a single platform running the entire length, accommodating 24 wagons. Cartage of goods and parcels at that time was in the hands of Messrs. Powlesland & Mason.

There were three sidings running through from the north to the south of the depot, one of which served the shed platform, all being stop-blocked at their southern ends. A further dead-end siding was provided at each end of the shed yard. Access to the shed yard at its north end was controlled from No. 4 Cabin (Maliphant box), on the east side of the line. No. 5 Cabin (North Dock Jct. box) was located opposite the south end of the goods yard, and controlled a ladder crossing from the line leading to the North Dock branch right across the running lines, and linking directly to all three of the 'through' goods yards sidings.

Opposite the goods shed, on the east side of the running lines, was a carriage works with two workshops, and a turntable with seven dead-end and three 'through' roads radiating off.

By 1898, the carriage works had been closed, and the area opposite the goods shed had been provided with ten carriage sidings and three goods sidings, while between Maliphant box and Hafod Junction, six further sidings had been laid in, part of which at least was shown as Messrs. Vivians Canal Head Sidings, these being taken over by the GWR by 1906.

Considerable expansion of facilities took place in 1906 with the opening of Hafod Yard, handling full load traffic with full cranage

and cartage facilities, to replace those previously provided at Swansea Goods. Also in that year, the poor quality of service offered to passengers between Swansea and West Wales was vastly improved. Travellers had formerly either to use the shuttle service between High Street and Landore, or proceed to Landore themselves, to connect with the through trains from Cardiff and London, with all the operating complications involved. To overcome this great inconvenience the Swansea Loop line was opened, providing a direct link between High Street (at Swansea Loop East) and the Landore to Cockett line, which was joined at Swansea Loop West. With most of the London and other services to and from the east of Cardiff too lengthy to be accommodated at the High Street platforms, the new link line was initially only used by local passenger services between Swansea and West Wales, and a few goods trains.

By the end of the Great War, the Great Western were using corridor bogie vehicles of up to 70 feet in length in their through trains, which had seen an ever-increasing number of vehicles on each service. The High Street station platforms were proving even more inadequate. So, in 1922, the GWR Board approved plans for the reconstruction of High Street station and additional facilities at the goods depot, involving the acquisition of a considerable area of land, the demolition of some dwelling houses and the closure and diversion of Powell Street.

Work began in 1923 on this ambitious project. First to be built were three new 900ft-long platforms with approach trackwork, providing two arrival and two departure faces, together with a fifth, shorter face (600ft), all carried by means of widened bridgework over the Strand, with parts of Jockey Street and Bargeman Row forming road junctions beneath platforms 1 and 2. Further, a subway from Pottery Street to the Strand was constructed under the station. The siding alongside the bay platform (No. 1) was used for

Landore 'Hall' No. 5913 *Rushton Hall* propelling the empty stock of the 12.45 p.m. Bristol to Swansea back towards the carriage sidings, in the distance, where other stock may be seen.

The down 10.55 a.m. Paddington 'Pembroke Coast Express' arriving at Swansea's platform 4 behind Landore 'Castle' No. 5039 *Rhuddlan Castle* on 30th April 1960. The train was due to arrive at 2.40 p.m., and the restaurant car portion was removed to travel back on the up 'PCE', which left at 3.45 p.m.; the car served lunch, tea and dinner during the day's roster. The down 'Pembroke Coast' was a fast train, calling only at Newport and Cardiff en route, with a journey time of 3 hrs 45 minutes to Swansea, and a scheduled formation of eight chocolate-and-cream coaches. On summer Saturdays it took thirty minutes more, due to a heavier load (four additional coaches, usually) and a heavier traffic pattern to contend with.

Canton 'Castle' No. 5073 *Blenheim* heading the five-coach 9.10 a.m. Manchester (London Road) to Swansea into platform 4 at High Street station on Saturday, 30th April 1960. The train had been reduced in length at Cardiff, where coaches from Manchester and Birkenhead were detached, leaving five vehicles to complete their journey.

No. 5062 *Earl of Shaftesbury* bringing a five-coach local service over the scissors crossover and into platform No. 2 at High Street in June 1961. The engine was transferred from Landore to Neath in June 1961, and was now carrying the latter's '87A' shedplate. 'Castle' No. 5062 carried the name *Tenby Castle* from new in June 1937 until November of that year, when the 'Earl' name from the '32XX' class of 4–4–0s was substituted. *Tenby Castle* was eventually carried by No. 7026 from new in 1949.

Pannier No. 9761 bringing a long rake of wagons cleared from Hafod Yard and Swansea Goods past High Street signal box on 30th April 1960, en route from the goods sidings to Eastern Depot via the North Dock branch. This line joined with and continued into the South Dock area on the Vale of Neath (ex-Swansea & Neath) line, running alongside the LMR Victoria station, and forming a junction with that line; a reversal was necessary to gain access to the main East Dock complex on the other side of the River Tawe. The goods shed, with the 1931 warehouse addition beyond, can be seen in the distance on the left.

No. 9404 with brake van coasting gently down the North Dock branch, to the rear of No. 5 platform, with the bulk of Kilvey Hill forming the backdrop. The North Docks branch was closed in 1965. F. K. DAVIES, CTY GW TRUST fish traffic. The previous pair of holding sidings for empty stock, etc., between platforms 3 and 4 were removed, and the area used to widen a new centre island platform. The lengthening of platforms, completed in 1926/7, enabled through services to and from West Wales to use High Street station as from 1926, and Landore's days of glory were over, only being served by stopping services from then on.

Work on the main station buildings commenced in the early 1930s. The main offices were positioned again on the departure (west) side, against platforms 1/2, curving around the corner to the south side; these included telegraph and parcels offices, cloak room, waiting rooms and toilets, and a tea room, with Divisional offices above. The main façade on the south side fronted on an enlarged Ivey Place, and contained the main booking offices with entrances

This photograph, taken in September 1948, shows the earlier arrangement of starting signals for platforms 3 to 5. In the background, a 'Grange' is seen manoeuvring a freight train on the spur alongside the docks line, with High Street box beyond.   J. CULL

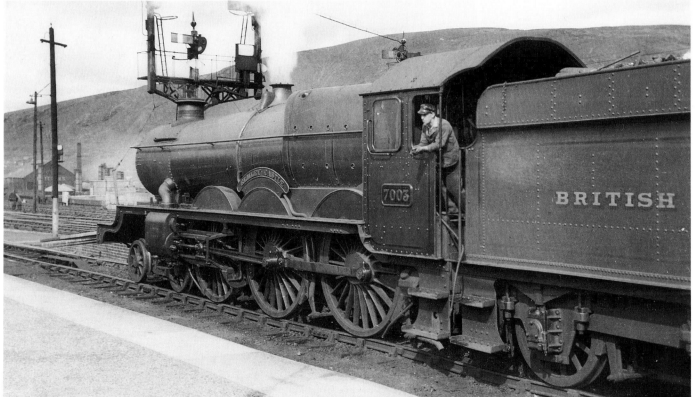

Landore 'Castle' No. 7003 *Elmley Castle* preparing to depart from platform 3 with an eastbound express on Saturday, 26th June 1948. This engine went new to Landore in June 1946 and remained there until December 1958 when she moved to Bath Road. During the late 1940s, No. 7003 was a regular visitor to Paddington with Welsh expresses, although she was also recorded arriving at that station with trains from Taunton and Weymouth, having doubtless been 'borrowed' by Old Oak to cover for engine failures before being permitted to return home. Some sheds, including Old Oak, traditionally had a number of engine diagrams that ran a short 'out and back' service before operating the outbound leg of a long-distance train later in the day, although these were of course subject to engine availability and other factors; often, a tank or a smaller tender engine was substituted.
F. K. DAVIES, CTY GW TRUST

Diesel railcar No. 4 running empty into Platform 2 at High Street to form the 9.35 a.m. service to Cheltenham on 8th July 1947.

H. C. CASSERLEY

on each side, leading straight through onto the circulating area across the ends of the platforms. Buildings were continued around the corner on the eastern ((No. 5) platform, and included the refreshment room and the gentlemen's toilets. Portland stonework was used on a Georgian style of architecture, with two floors to each side, and three on the main facade.

The cramped approaches to the goods facilities off High Street and alongside the passenger station were swept away, and a new road was built from Prince of Wales Road, running eastwards on an embankment along the site of Bethesda Street, across the Upper Strand by a 30ft-high bridge, and into the southern end of the yard. The northern end of the goods shed itself was demolished, and a new three-storey concrete warehouse was constructed, 200ft long and 52ft wide, through the ground floor of which the original goods platform was extended.

A locomotive yard was constructed against the eastern side of the station, off the North Docks branch, where engines could be turned and watered. The turntable as installed was 55ft diameter. This provided the ability for a quick turn-round, rather than running out to Landore.

Landore 'Castle' No. 5093 *Upton Castle* at platform No. 3 with the 7.30 a.m. Carmarthen to Paddington service on 8th July 1947, due to depart at 8.50 a.m. non-stop to Cardiff (depart 10.0 a.m.). This train would, in 1950, become the up 'Red Dragon'. No. 5093 was at Landore between March 1941 and June 1952, and in this last year of the company's existence, had been turned out in fine condition for this turn.
H. C. CASSERLEY

Landore 'Castle' No. 4081 *Warwick Castle* waiting for the road at the end of platform No. 2 for the run up to Landore after working a stopping service into Swansea on 11th May 1953. The engine is seen here still carrying a lamp in the 'B' class position, but would doubtless have carried another over the bufferbeam on its tender for the light engine movement.
T .J. EDGINGTON

The view from the north end of platform 5 at Swansea High Street as the 1.30 p.m. Swansea to Paddington (11.10 a.m. Milford Haven) was departing from platform 2 behind its returning Old Oak Common 'Castle' on Saturday, 30th April 1960. The train conveyed through coaches from both Milford and Pembroke Dock, as well as a dining car portion from Swansea. On leaving the station, northbound trains towards Loop East Jct. had a half-mile of favourable gradients before reaching the climb to either Landore or Loop West.

Local services progressively disappeared during the 1960s from Swansea High Street. The Morriston Branch service was discontinued in 1962, Rhondda & Swansea Bay services (from Treherbert) in 1964, the Porthcawl service in 1965, and the Vale of Neath services (some of which ran through to Swansea, reversing at Neath) in 1965, leaving eastbound trains to Cardiff calling only at Neath, Port Talbot and Bridgend, and westbound trains at Llanelly and Carmarthen before proceeding to principal stations in West Wales.

Until summer 1963, Paddington services had normally detached and attached the restaurant car portion at Swansea, with London services to the west of Swansea being composed of six or seven coaches. From September 1963, in the interest of coach utilisation, London services terminated at Swansea, with a fresh diesel-hauled service beyond, mostly with DMUs.

Various sidings were recovered during the rationalisation exercises of the late 1960s and early 70s, but in 1972 the disengagement

Having been released from her train, Landore 'Castle' No. 5039 *Rhuddlan Castle* is seen reversing past the signal at the end of Platform 4 en route to Landore shed on Saturday, 30th April 1960. This was Landore No. 1 turn, which commenced with the 2.30 p.m. Neyland to Paddington (5.30 p.m. ex-Swansea), returning to Swansea with the 'PCE', 10.55 a.m. Paddington, the following morning.

Landore 'Castle' No. 4093 *Dunster Castle* reversing out from platform 4 with empty coaches to carriage sidings on 26th September 1959. The lower arm on the bracket signal was 'off', and the movement identified on the indicator alongside it. No. 4093 received its double chimney in December 1957, one of the earlier 'Castles' to be fitted.

F. K. DAVIES, CTY GW TRUST

The 1.5 p.m. Pembroke Dock to Paddington – the 'Pembroke Coast Express' – arriving at platform 4 behind Landore 'Castle' No. 5013, *Abergavenny Castle* on Saturday, 30th April 1960. The train (other than the leading, strengthening vehicle) was in chocolate and cream livery, appropriately identified by the letters 'GWR' in *Through Coach Working Programmes* of the period. Although top-link, low-mileage Landore 'Castles' were mainly used on the London services, the higher-mileage engines worked to Cardiff, Llanelly, Carmarthen, Whitland and Fishguard on a daily basis. The southern end of High Street goods can be seen to the left, fenced off at this point.

The restaurant car portion had been attached to the front, and the engine, Old Oak Common Castle No. 4096 *Highclere Castle*, was ready to depart with the 1.5 p.m. Pembroke Dock train on 30th April 1960. The headboard and reporting number were used only between Paddington and Swansea, but the headboard was carried between Carmarthen and Pembroke Dock. The service was due into Paddington at 7.45 p.m., although on summer Saturdays it was due at 8.25 p.m., with a rather more leisurely schedule after Cardiff, and additional calls at Slough and Ealing Broadway to set down passengers.

Departure: an atmospheric view of No. 4096 taking the up 'PCE' train out of platform 4, with passengers waving from the windows of the leading Van Second. A four-coach set, including the dining car, was usually attached to the front at Swansea in the winter months. Roof boards displaying 'Paddington, Newport, Cardiff and Swansea' on these coaches were the standard style for the through vehicles, showing the route, though not indicating a direction of travel (so they would be appropriate for both directions), whilst the traditional boards for Pembroke were written 'Paddington, Tenby and Pembroke Dock'. Some named trains also carried boards with the title. A 'Tenby and Carmarthen Bay Express' was also current in one period during the 1930s.

Looking along platform No. 1 towards the buffer stops, c.1962; this platform would be taken out of use in 1973, and the trackwork removed. The fish siding can be seen diverging from the platform road, with glimpses of the rear of the 1930s station building above the No. 1 platform canopy, and the older buildings to its right.

LENS OF SUTTON

Landore 'Hall' No. 5923 *Colston Hall* alongside platform 2 with the 10.15 a.m. Carmarthen (11.30 a.m. Swansea) to Gloucester and Cheltenham on Monday, 11th May 1953. The basic set of four coaches was formed Van Third, Composite, Third and Van Third, corridor stock, to which was usually added a 'Siphon' from Carmarthen to Cardiff, probably at the rear in this view. The stock had started that morning as the 8.0 a.m. to Carmarthen, and would return home as the 8.40 p.m. from Cardiff. Nearby, the Swansea dining car portion of the next up London service (departing at 1.30 p.m.) was being held in Platform I.

T J. EDGINGTON

from goods sundries ('smalls') traffic caused the eventual closure of Swansea Goods. A similar withdrawal in 1976 from wagon-load traffic removed most of the traffic from Hafod Yard, though in both cases the sidings were not lifted until 1983.

From October 1973, the No. 1 Bay platform at High Street was taken out of use, and the remaining platforms renumbered 1 to 4. At the same time, the previous Down Relief Line became a Down Goods Loop, though it is difficult to see what goods traffic was now involved!

Maliphant Sidings became an important maintenance and heavy cleaning yard for coaching stock, especially after the 1963 change

from portion working on the Paddington & West Wales services to fixed formations on the new Paddington & Swansea, when several train sets were allocated to Maliphant.

From 1976, High Speed Trains were introduced on the Paddington to Swansea service with Maliphant still involved in servicing, and the Swansea restaurant car staff employed on many trains throughout the day as they had done in previous years of portion working. Gradually, a few trains at the start and end of the day started back from or terminated at Carmarthen, to again offer what was previously a popular through journey potential.

No. 7021 *Haverfordwest Castle* departing from No. 2 platform with the 3.10 p.m. to Paddington on Sunday, 9th September 1951. The engine was from Landore shed, although the following year this turn was scheduled for an Old Oak 'Castle', a return working of the Sunday 12.50 a.m. Paddington to Swansea newspaper train.

Having previously worked the 12.45 a.m. Paddington newspaper and sleeping car train from Cardiff to Swansea, Canton 'Britannia' No. 70024 *Vulcan* is seen alongside platform 2 with the 11.30 a.m. departure for Paddington (A64) on Monday, 13th June 1960; this high-mileage engine would have changed at Cardiff for a recently ex-works 'Britannia' or 'Castle' for the journey onwards to London. This was the first day of the summer timetable, and the first use of the combined letter and numbers system of train identification, in this instance 'A64' for the 8.30 a.m. Pembroke Dock.   F. K. DAVIES, CTY GW TRUST

Neath '94XX' o-6-oPT No.9446 at platform 3 on
Monday, 20th June 1955 with a local service, possibly
the 4.50 p.m. train from High Street to Treherbert.
This train was composed of a four-coach local set,
with strengthening or tail traffic as required.

F. K. DAVIES, CTY GW TRUST

The Landore 'treatment' is very apparent in this view
of the beautifully-clean, and now-preserved, 'Castle'
No. 5051 *Earl Bathurst*, at the head of the up 'South
Wales Pullman' at platform 3, awaiting departure at
4.35 p.m., during the summer of 1959. The engine
turn was Landore 2, and it would return with the
8.55 a.m. Paddington to Pembroke Dock train the
following morning.

F. K. DAVIES, CTY GW TRUST

On 25th September 1965, Tondu pannier No. 9609 is seen at platform 2 with a joint RCTS/SLS special. H.C. CASSERLEY

This picture of Landore 'Hall' No. 6903 *Belmont Hall*, standing at platform 4 with a morning local departure on Monday, 17th June 1957, shows the curvature of the track in the central section of the station. The platforms at High Street – with the exception of No. 1 – were between 888ft (No. 5) and 934ft (No. 4) in length, though trains entering the station were limited to 870 feet (including the engine). The longer island platform (3/4) accommodated train engines at both ends. Again, a restaurant car portion is apparent at the adjacent platform face.
F. K. DAVIES, CTY GW TRUST

A view northwards along Nos. 3/4 platforms in early 1949, with 'Hall' No. 5976 *Ashwicke Hall* from St. Philip's Marsh shed alongside No. 2 platform with an arrival; the rather deserted look to the station might suggest a Sunday, and the train could therefore have been the 11.26 a.m. from Swindon, conveying through coaches from the 9.20 a.m. Paddington. This engine had recently been reconverted back for coal burning after some 18 months as an oil burner (numbered 3951).
NATIONAL RAILWAY MUSEUM

'Landore Hall' No. 5913 *Rushton Hall* at platform 5 on Saturday, 30th April 1960 with the empty stock of the 12.43 p.m. Bristol to Swansea, which she would shortly propel out to the carriage sidings just outside the station. This train was a semi-fast, calling at principal stations, but also at Stapleton Road, Llantrisant and Pyle. Platform 5 was the easternmost platform at High Street, behind which ran the goods line to North Dock.

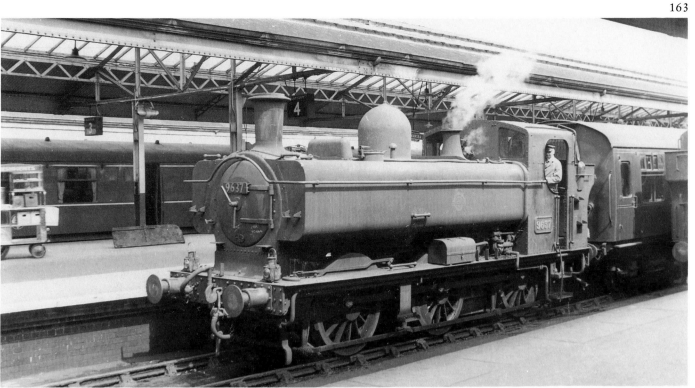

Landore 'Pannier' tank No. 9637 on station pilot duty with ECS to the carriage sidings on the morning of 23rd June 1960. The engine was carrying not 'A' headlamps, but one white and one red lamp to denote station pilot duty
F. K. DAVIES, CTY GW TRUST

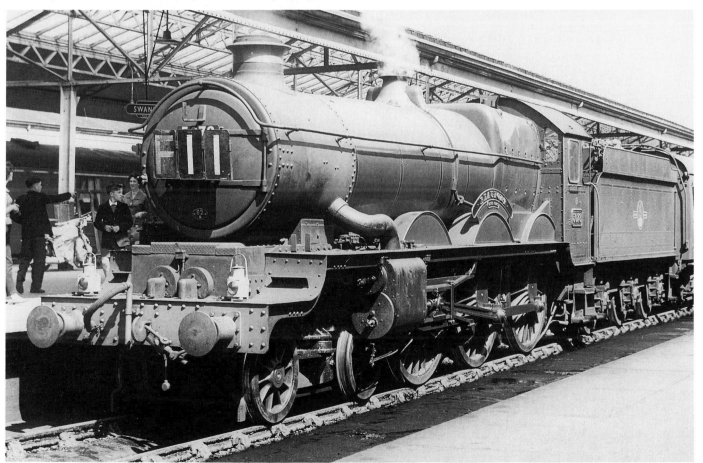

Bath Road 'Castle' No. 5078 *Beaufort* at platform 2 with the recently-arrived 7.55 a.m. service from Paddington to Pembroke Dock in June 1960. This was a Landore duty (Turn 3) from Paddington to Swansea, the return of the previous day's 2.30 p.m. Swansea (12.5 p.m. Milford), but on this occasion a Bristol engine had found its way onto the train.
G. W. SHARPE COLLECTION

When the 'Blue Pullman' commenced operations in September 1961, the 'Capitals United Express' ceased to run as the 6.30 a.m. Swansea to Paddington and the 3.55 return and instead became the 8.55 a.m. down and 1.30 p.m. ex-Swansea (11.10 a.m. Milford Haven). This view shows Neath 'Castle' No. 4099 *Kilgerran Castle* at platform 4, with the recently-arrived 8.55 a.m. Paddington train (due 1.25 p.m.), formed of chocolate and cream Mark 1 stock, in spring 1962. This engine had moved from Penzance to Landore in November 1957, and remained in the Swansea area for the rest of her days.

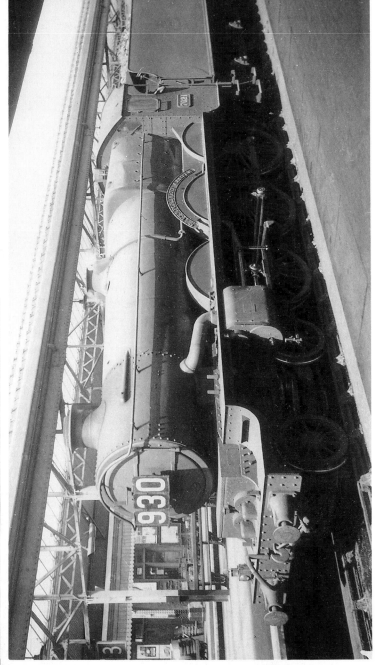

After an 18-month gap, the Western Region recommenced the building programme for 'Castles' in early 1948, with No. 7008 (*Swansea Castle*) entering traffic in May of that year. Here Landore 'Castle' No. 7021 *Haverfordwest Castle*, then two years old, is seen at the head of the 8.55 a.m. Paddington to Pembroke Dock (train No. 930) in platform 4 on Thursday, 19th June 1951. No. 7021 remained at Landore until November 1957 when she moved to Carmarthen, returning to Landore in June 1959, and moving to Llanelly when Landore closed for dieselisation.

F. K. DAVIES, CTY GW TRUST

Only 10 months old, Landore 'Castle' No. 7028 *Cadbury Castle* is seen at platform 4 at the head of the 8.55 a.m. Paddington to Pembroke Dock (train No. 930) arrival on Tuesday, 17th April 1951. At this time, the reporting numbers for trains from Paddington to Cheltenham or South Wales fell into the 810–855 sequence, with up trains in the 930–970 series, these having been generally current since 1946. For 1952, these were changed to 161–179 and 710–755 respectively, the increasing numbers of through holiday trains from and to the Midlands taking up the previous, higher reporting numbers.

F. K. DAVIES, CTY GW TRUST

Landore 'Hall' No. 5923 *Colston Hall* with an arriving stopper at platform 3 on the afternoon of Thursday, 17th April 1952. The 'Halls' from Landore did most of their passenger work to Cardiff or Gloucester in the east, and Carmarthen or Whitland to the west, including parcels and milk services. The restaurant car portion of a Paddington express can be seen at platform 4. F. K. DAVIES, CTY GW TRUST

'Grange' No. 6852 *Headbourne Grange* of Bristol (St. Philip's Marsh) had just arrived with a service at platform 4 on the morning of Monday, 13th June 1960, carrying the single lamp on the bufferbeam in readiness for a movement out of the station. At this time, Carmarthen and St. Philip's Marsh sheds alternated on a mixed traffic 4–6–0 duty involving fast freights between those two places, with a fill-in return trip hauling two West Wales expresses from Carmarthen (12.5 p.m. Milford) and Swansea (11.55 p.m. Paddington) before taking the 9.0 p.m. Carmarthen freight back to Bristol.

F.K. DAVIES,
CTY GW TRUST

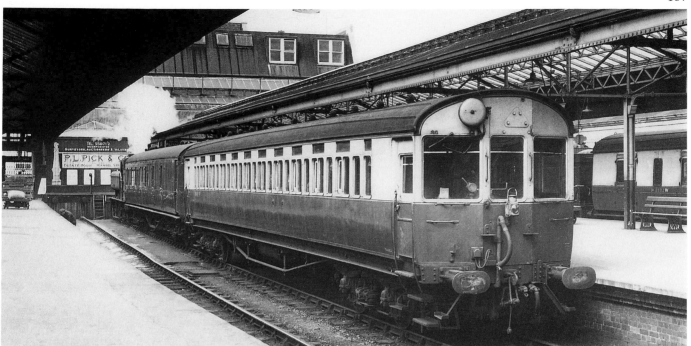

This picture, taken on Wednesday, 3rd June 1953, shows the 10.20 a.m. auto service to Llanelly and Carmarthen awaiting departure from No. 4 platform. The experimental trailer No. 48 was originally constructed in 1907 to gain some experience of high-capacity cars on suburban services, with sliding doors operated remotely by the guard. It was rebuilt in 1912 into a more conventional trailer, with panelling in place of the sliding doors, and with saloons in place of the open design. Trailer W48W was accompanied here by compartment Trailer Van Third No. 1670, the pair being propelled by Landore '64XX' No. 6431.

R. C. RILEY/THE TRANSPORT TREASURY

A Vale of Neath service from Pontypool Road alongside platform 4 behind Swansea East Dock 0–6–2T No. 6680 – which had worked the train from Neath on Saturday, 18th August 1962. Trains generally took between 145 and 165 minutes for the 49½-mile journey, serving up to 26 intermediate stations en route. Tank engines were almost always used for passenger duties on the Vale of Neath, although 2–6–0s and 4–6–0s did appear from time to time between Pontypool Road and Neath, whilst 4–6–0s were also to be seen on excursion traffic. The water bowser on the left was used for filling coach reservoirs.

F. K. DAVIES, CITY GW TRUST

Railcar W13 at No. 5 platform, High Street station, on arrival from Paddington with an LRTL special on Sunday, 28th September 1952. The car returned to Paddington on the same day, a round journey of at least 380 miles. Another special, made a year later by the car from Paddington to Towyn and back, was scheduled for some 455 miles, though it broke down at Lapworth on its return.   E. D. BRUTON

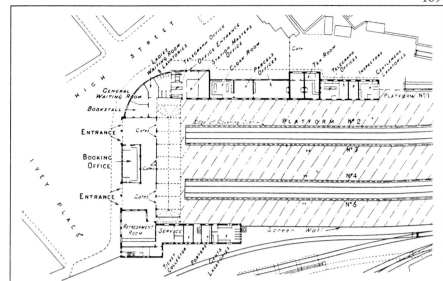

*The layout of the offices and other facilities
at the new Swansea High Street station.*
RAILWAY GAZETTE

Though there were two London Midland stations at Swansea (St. Thomas, ex-Midland, and Victoria, ex-L & NW), appearances by LMR engines were very rare at High Street. An event which produced one, however, was an SLS special to the Swansea Vale and other local lines on Saturday, 14th July 1956, part of which brought 0–6–0T No. 47479 into the station with the two-coach formation.
T .J. EDGINGTON

Diesel railcar No. 4 alongside platform 2 with the 9.35 a.m. service to Cheltenham on 8th July 1947. This buffet car service ran non-stop to Cardiff, then called at Newport, Chepstow, Lydney, Newnham and Gloucester (due 12.18 p.m.), where it stayed for some fifty minutes before proceeding to Cheltenham. Passengers for Cheltenham would need to change at Gloucester into the 12.33 p.m. passenger for a prompt service onwards. The return diesel trip departed from Cheltenham at 2.15 p.m., calling at Gloucester, Chepstow (to pick up only), Newport and Cardiff en route, and was due into Swansea at 5.51 p.m. At this time, Landore had an allocation of cars Nos. 2, 4 and 16.
H. C. CASSERLEY

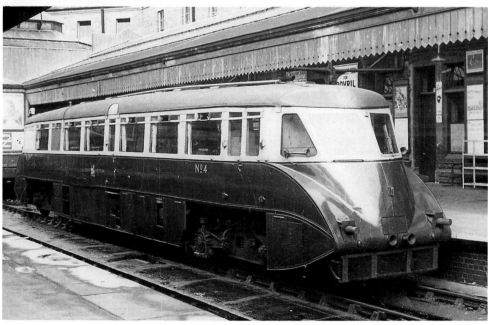

Engines awaiting their incoming trains frequently stood at the end of the North Dock branch, in the position occupied by Old Oak Common 'Castle' No. 4006 *Highclere Castle* destined for the up 'Pembroke Coast Express' (3.45 p.m. ex-Swansea) on Saturday, 30th April 1960. The turn was OOC 25, which the 'Castle' had worked the previous night on the 8.55 p.m. Paddington to Neyland as far as Swansea. The view clearly shows the High Street signal box, with the goods and carriage sidings beyond.

Carmarthen-based 'Castle' No. 5030 *Shirburn Castle* at the station end of the North Dock branch with a passenger brake van on 30th April 1960. Before its working back to Carmarthen, it would have run the short distance down the North Dock line to the turntable, located alongside the station. This engine was only ever based at four sheds: new in June 1934, she first went to Exeter, then in May 1936 to Canton, to Ebbw Jct. between March 1941 and August 1942, returning to Canton, and finally in August 1958 to Carmarthen. She was withdrawn in September 1962 and sold as scrap to R.S. Hayes at Bridgend.

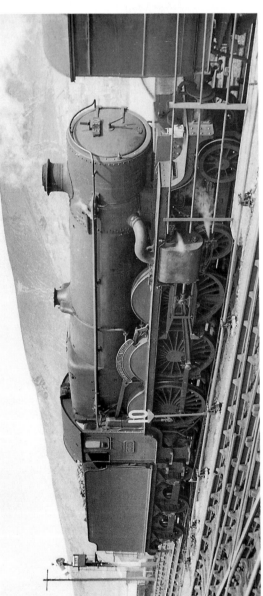

As part of the station reconstruction scheme of the mid-1920s, a 55ft turntable sufficient for types up to and including 'Castles' was installed at the station end of the North Dock branch in an area already occupied by sidings, to save engines having to run to Landore to turn – particularly those on short runs from and to Carmarthen. Landore shed was supplied with a 65ft turntable, whilst the option of turning on Landore triangle was also available. In this view, Landore 'Castle' No. 5091 *Cleeve Abbey* and a 'Hall' had already been turned, and are seen in front of the turntable on 15th September 1962. The rear wall of platform 5 can be seen to the right, whilst the docks branch passed the position occupied by the photographer.

R. O. TUCK

ACKNOWLEDGEMENTS

My thanks go to John Copsey for his usual weighty contribution to the production of this volume, to Richard Woodley for his valuable comments, and to John Mann for his engineering expertise. I am grateful to the GW Trust for permission to use F. K. Davies and other prints from their collection, to Brian Stephenson and Keith Jones for the R. O. Tuck and Sid Rickard material, and to various national dealers and others for support material; also to Tony Cooke whose invaluable *Track Layout Diagrams* and *Atlas* have, as usual, been religiously consulted. I have also referred to the August 1960 *Railway Magazine* article on Margam Yard and J. N. Westwood's article on Swansea High Street in *Trains Illustrated*, February 1956. Great use has also been made of service timetables and appendices, engine diagrams, coach working programmes freight marshalling and other operational documentation, and of course that excellent reference work, the *Great Western Magazine*.

John Hodge

Harry Potter
AND THE HALF-BLOOD PRINCE

Alfred Music Publishing Co., Inc.
16320 Roscoe Blvd., Suite 100
P.O. Box 10003
Van Nuys, CA 91410-0003
alfred.com

ISBN-10: 0-7390-6167-4
ISBN-13: 978-0-7390-6167-1

CONTENTS

IN NOCTEM

Lyrics by
STEVE KLOVES

Music by
NICHOLAS HOOPER

In Noctem - 4 - 1
32863

day.

Men: *lontano (chanting)*

p Fer - te in noc - tem a - ni - mam

me - am I - lust - rent stel - lae vi - am me - am As - pec - tu

i - llo glo - ri - or Dum ca - pit nox___ di -

6

GINNY

By NICHOLAS HOOPER

WIZARD WHEEZES

By NICHOLAS HOOPER

FAREWELL ARAGOG

By NICHOLAS HOOPER

Moderately slow ♩ = 76

(with pedal)

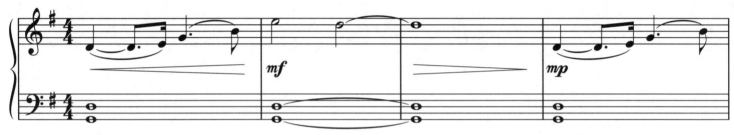

Farewell Aragog - 2 - 1
32863

HARRY AND HERMIONE

By NICHOLAS HOOPER

WHEN GINNY KISSED HARRY

By NICHOLAS HOOPER

Gentle and lilting ♩. = 56

(with pedal)

When Ginny Kissed Harry - 3 - 1
32863

DUMBLEDORE'S FAREWELL

By NICHOLAS HOOPER

Moderately slow, expressively ♩ = 96

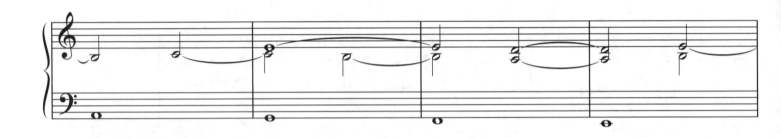

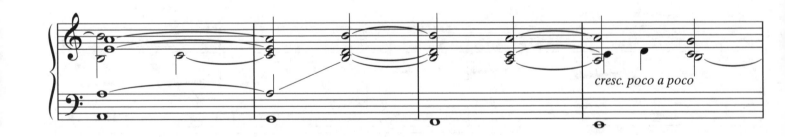

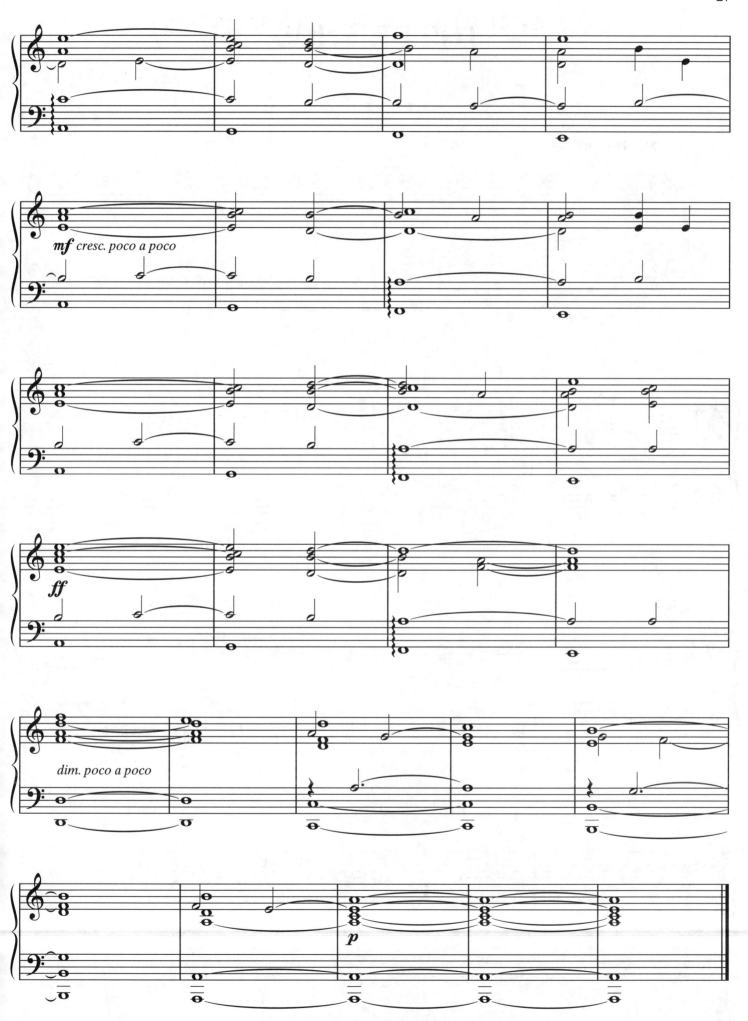

THE FRIENDS

By NICHOLAS HOOPER

Slowly ♩ = 69

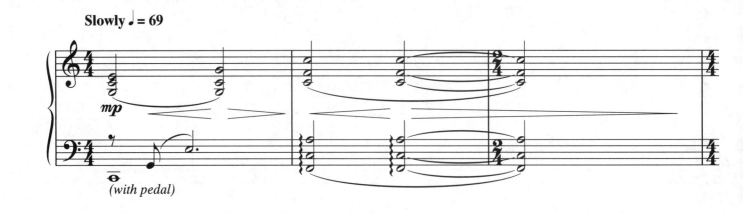

The Friends - 2 - 1
32863

THE WEASLEY STOMP

By NICHOLAS HOOPER

SLUGHORN'S CONFESSION

By NICHOLAS HOOPER

Slughorn's Confession - 3 - 1
32863

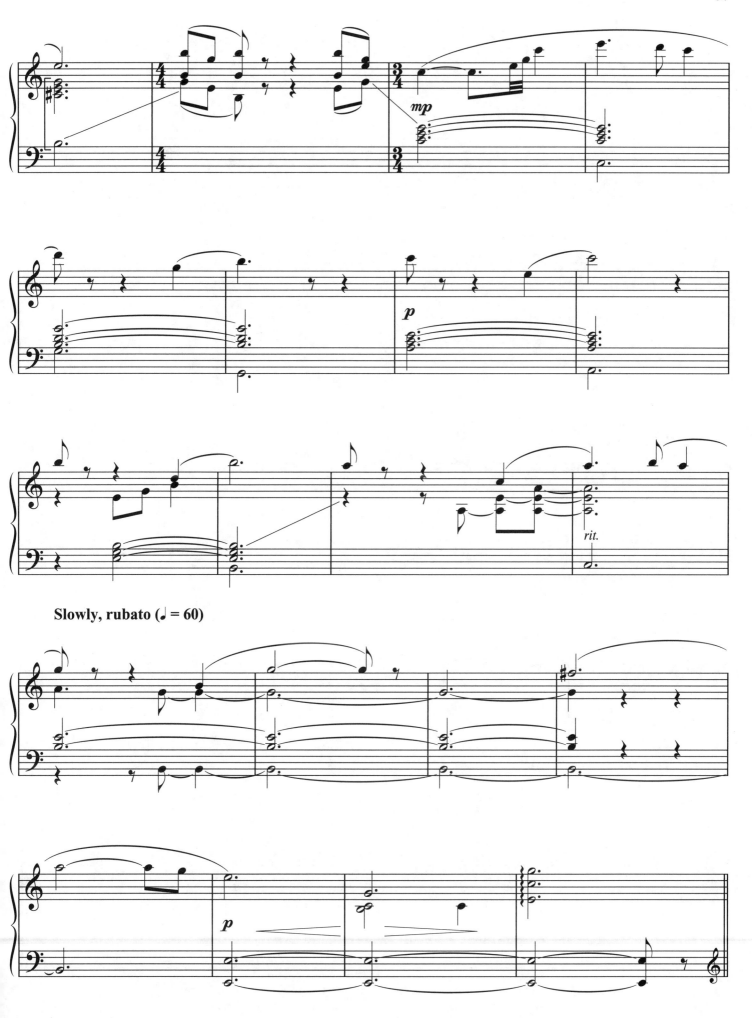

Slowly, rubato (♩ = 60)